Essential
Venice

by
TOM POCOCK

Tom Pocock has visited Venice many times as a foreign correspondent and travel writer and on holiday. Formerly on the staff of the *Daily Mail*, *Daily Express* and *The Times* and travel editor of the *Evening Standard*, he now contributes travel articles to *The Times* and *The Guardian*. He is author of 11 books, most of them historical biographies.

AA

Produced by AA Publishing

Written by Tom Pocock
Peace and Quiet section
by Paul Sterry

Reprinted November 1995
Revised second edition January 1995
First published January 1991

Edited, designed and produced by AA Publishing.
© The Automobile Association 1995.
Maps © The Automobile Association 1995.

Distributed in the United Kingdom by AA Publishing, Norfolk House, Priestley Road, Basingstoke, Hampshire, RG24 9NY.

A CIP catalogue record for this book is available from the British Library.

ISBN 0 7495 0920 1

The contents of this publication are believed correct at the time of printing. Nevertheless, the publishers cannot be held responsible for any errors or omissions or for changes in the details given in this guide or for the consequences of any reliance on the information provided by the same. Assessments of attractions, hotels, restaurants and so forth are based upon the author's own experience and, therefore, descriptions given in this guide necessarily contain an element of subjective opinion which may not reflect the publisher's opinion or dictate a reader's own experience on another occasion. **We have tried to ensure accuracy in this guide, but things do change and we would be grateful if readers would advise us of any inaccuracies they may encounter.**

Published by AA Publishing, a trading name of Automobile Association Developments Limited, whose registered office is Norfolk House, Priestley Road, Basingstoke, Hampshire, RG24 9NY.
Registered number 1878835.

Colour separation: Mullis Morgan Ltd, London.

Printed by: Printers Trento, S.R.L., Italy

Front cover picture: The Grand Canal

INTRODUCTION 4

BACKGROUND 8

WHAT TO SEE IN VENICE 17

EXCURSIONS FROM
VENICE 57

PEACE AND QUIET
Countryside and Wildlife
in and around Venice 69

FOOD AND DRINK 77

SHOPPING 83

ACCOMMODATION 89

CULTURE, ENTERTAINMENT
AND NIGHTLIFE 96

WEATHER AND
WHEN TO GO 97

HOW TO BE A LOCAL 98

PERSONAL PRIORITIES 100

CHILDREN 101

TIGHT BUDGET 101

SPECIAL EVENTS 102

SPORT 104

DIRECTORY 105

LANGUAGE 121

INDEX 126

Maps and Plans

Italy	4
Venézia-Sestieri	16–17
Venézia	18–19
Canal Grande	24–25
Laguna Véneta	58
Venézia Excursions	67

This book employs a simple
rating system to help choose
which places to visit:

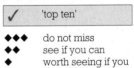

| ✓ | 'top ten' |

◆◆◆	do not miss
◆◆	see if you can
◆	worth seeing if you have time

INTRODUCTION

Venice is the most extraordinary and
beautiful city in the world. That claim is as
difficult to dispute as that which describes it
as the greatest work of art yet created. This
view encompasses the architecture, the art,
its setting in water and a history which has
given the city a haunting atmosphere evoking
the magnificence of its past.

The first sight of Venice comes as a shock of
surprise and delight, whether the city is
seen from the steps of the railway station, or
from an airport water-taxi when it suddenly
bursts from a canal into the sunlit splendours
of the Grand Canal or the Basin of San Marco.
Such intense pleasure will be felt often over
the coming days and be enhanced by

The tranquillity of sunset on the Grand Canal: time to reflect as the water turns to silken pinks and blues

repeated visits. Sometimes it will be a view: sunset behind the dome of the Salute; the moon above the island of San Giorgio; the rising or setting sun turning the water of the lagoon to a silken pink, blue and gold; the whole city, seen from an approaching boat, seeming to rise from the blue and white of sea and haze.

Or it may be a sudden glimpse of a painted, candlelit ceiling; reflections of Gothic arches in the still water of a canal; cloaked figures in masks and tricorn hats seen in the fog at the time of the winter carnival; gondolas dipping across water dancing with reflected light; even snow on the Rialto.

What is most remarkable is that others, who lived centuries ago, have experienced the same excitement because they saw what you are seeing. Look at the paintings of Venice by Canaletto and, apart from the clothes of the Venetians, they might have been painted today and not in the 18th century. Even the Venice of five centuries ago is instantly recognisable in paintings and maps.

No wonder it has enchanted visitors – not only beguiling the eye but bewitching the mind – for so long. Charles Dickens described his own visit in 1844 as if it were a strange and beautiful dream. He ended his account of

INTRODUCTION

A string of colourful sun shades makes the restaurants along Riva del Vin ideal for lunch by the Ponte di Rialto

experiences we can still share: 'I have, many and many a time, thought since of this strange dream upon the water: half-wondering if it lie there yet, and if its name be Venice'. Today his wonder is echoed by a small child's bemused question on arrival for a family holiday: 'Daddy, is the water *meant?*'

A few will complain that they did not enjoy a first visit to Venice: it was hot and crowded; there were smells from the canals and mosquitoes at night. Do not be put off. Of course, it can be hot and there may be mosquitoes in summer as is the case throughout these latitudes. There can be watery smells and, again in summer, an occasional whiff of something worse, but that is rare. Yes, it can be crowded – sometimes too crowded in season – but Venice was designed to cope with crowds.

The character of Venice is complex. Yet through the glorious colours of this great

historical tapestry runs a sinister thread. In the days of its wealth and power, its opulence had a counterpoint in the secret denunciations of real or imagined traitors. In its last century of independence, Venice was ripe with decadence. Even today, despite mass tourism and great international exhibitions, the city remains secretive; few of its palaces are open to the public and hospitality is usually on a business basis. It is strangely quirky, even haunted, and the visitor can feel that past Venetians are never far away; but probably that is just the effect of shadows and reflections.

Perhaps the most remarkable of all its qualities is this sense of unity with the past. The history of Venice stretches back for over a thousand years but its parentage – the civilisations of Rome, Greece and even Egypt – goes back to the beginning of the recorded activity of mankind.

BACKGROUND

History

Venice is a survivor and always was. A thousand years ago, it was the only survivor of the Ancient World to escape the Dark Ages. The first Venetians were refugees. When the barbarian invasions from the north and east streamed across the plains of northern Italy, burning the towns and shattering the order of the Roman Empire, a few of those who escaped massacre or slavery took refuge among the reed-beds, mud-banks and islands where the rivers from the distant Alps flow into the Adriatic.

This happened in the 5th and 6th centuries after Christ. At first the fugitives lived in camps, then in settlements that grew to villages; finally these became ordered into large communities and sought the protection of the principal survivor of the Roman world, Byzantium. Until the 10th century, Venice was loosely subject to the Byzantine emperor. But it had already learned to stand on its own feet on those remote islands, particularly after its own victory over an attempted invasion by the son of the Holy Roman Emperor Charlemagne in AD810. A few years later the body of St Mark was smuggled from Alexandria to the main settlement, now moved from Torcello, near the mainland shore, to the more distant and secure Rialto islands.

Since AD742, the Venetians had elected their own head of state, the Doge, and gradually a constitution evolved. Already semi-independent, the Venetians used their Byzantine connections to trade with the East and to develop their capacity to trade by sea. The growth of wealth made it important to limit individual power, particularly of the Doge himself, so in 1172 a Great Council of nearly 500 Venetians was formed, and from this grew an elaborate system of executive responsibility to ensure that no individual or faction became dominant in the administration of what was now the Venetian Republic. Venice became the principal link between Europe and the East and not only in trade. Venetian ships were chartered for transporting armies to fight in the Crusades, and the Venetians themselves sent an army to capture and sack their former source of protection and patronage, Byzantium (the great maritime city that was later to be known as Constantinople and then Istanbul). The Venetians also confronted their rival sea power, Genoa, and triumphed. While establishing its dominance of the Mediterranean, the Republic founded an empire, which stretched down the Dalmatian coast of the Adriatic to the Greek islands, Crete and Cyprus. Meanwhile, Venice expanded into its own hinterland as far north as the Alps and almost as far west as Milan. A new threat had arisen: the Turks of the aggressive Ottoman Empire. In 1453, the Turks had stormed and sacked Constantinople and were moving westward across the Mediterranean and into Europe. One by one, the Venetian colonies and castles fell during the course of a century. At the same time, the Venetians were having to defend themselves against European rivals. Venice itself survived thanks to a combination of

Michele Steno, one of 25 Doge buried in the church known as San Zanipolo

BACKGROUND

Carnival time and the whole city celebrates: Venetian masks add intrigue to the fantastic colourful costumes

military and diplomatic skill but not before most of its empire had been lost to the Turks. The Republic might have regained its former power had not the context of its success radically changed. Trade with the East could now flow round the Cape of Good Hope by sea rather than by overland caravans to Mediterranean ports as it had formerly. Trade with the Americas had begun and other Europeans were at last challenging Venetian pre-eminence in trading. The great days of Venice were ending but it was still immensely rich and by the beginning of the 18th century, its merchants and aristocracy were concentrating on enjoying their money. Venice was known as the decadent pleasure-city of Europe, famous for its carnivals, gambling, masked balls, prostitution and a sensual enjoyment of the arts.

The Republic was ripe for plundering when, in 1797, Napoleon and his Revolutionary army swept into Italy, seized the city and deposed the last of its 120 Doges. The French gave Venice to the Austrians, who defeated a patriotic rebellion in 1848, regaining control until 1866 when Venice was finally united with

Italy. For the next 60 years, Venice remained a beautiful relic of past glories. Then, between the two world wars, the industrial development of Marghera and Mestre on the mainland at the head of the causeway to Venice was begun. This provided employment for Venetians but it also produced pollution of the atmosphere by corroding fumes that have damaged the fragile fabric of the ancient city across the water.

The tapping of underground water led to subsidence in the city and, when that was stopped, there came the threat of high tides sweeping into the lagoon along the deep, dredged shipping channels leading to the new commercial port. Now comes the threat of a probable rise in sea-levels caused by the 'greenhouse effect' of man-made gases in the stratosphere.

After the floods of 1966, those who loved Venice raised relief funds to restore individual buildings, if not save the city itself. Finally the Italian government planned to control the flow of the tides through the three entrances to the lagoon with huge, movable barriers but, it was feared, this would not be enough to counter the calamity threatened by the world-wide rise in sea-levels.

A more immediate danger is that of invasion by tourists. By 1990, the city was crowded with as many as 25,000 visitors a day in summer and, in 1989, more than 200,000 poured into it for a pop music concert and most stayed overnight in the square and alleys, creating such havoc that one Venetian declared that the city had been raped. But just as schemes to limit the crowds, and the damage they inevitably cause, were being discussed, proposals were made to hold the gigantic Expo 2000 trade fair and festival on the nearby mainland. This, it was estimated, would bring a quarter of a million visitors into Venice every day while it lasted.

Architecture and Art

No city in the world can offer such richness in art and architecture as Venice, where the ethos of the Ancient World combined with the

Venice by night: the Palazzo Ducale and the Campanile di S Marco seem to rise straight from the depths of the lagoon

inflow of taste and ideas from the East to fertilise the imaginations and taste of some of the richest and most powerful people in Europe. Centuries of such cross-fertilisation have created a city that is unlike anywhere else.

As buildings of brick and stone replaced those of mud and wattle, wooden piles were sunk in the mud to support foundations: millions of them, so that the hills along the Adriatic coasts were stripped of trees. The earliest influence on the emerging architecture was Byzantine – that blend of the Roman with the oriental – and this can be seen both in the Basilica di San Marco and the cathedral of Torcello which was built around the year AD1000 and is said to be the oldest Venetian building. The buildings were often adorned with marble, columns and decoration imported from Constantinople.

The Byzantine merged with the Gothic to
produce the most characteristic architecture
of the city. In the 14th and 15th centuries this
gave Venice great buildings like the Doges'
Palace and the Ca' d'Oro which managed to
combine nobility and frivolity.

This in turn merged with the Renaissance style
– the revival of classical principles in
architecture – and added a magnificence to
churches and palaces, which is best seen at a
distance. The baroque and rococo influences
of the 17th and 18th centuries added
sensuality to the mixture of styles until
Napoleon's extinction of the Republic in 1797
put an end to purely Venetian evolution.
Thereafter, the invaders' neoclassical taste
was introduced here and there, as was that of
the later Austrian occupiers.

Venetian painting, as it evolved over four
centuries, was remarkable for its luminous,

sensual quality that reflected the Venetians'
enjoyment of life. Several of the most
celebrated painters of the Venetian School
belonged to families that produced
generations of artists – the Bellinis, the
Vivarinis and the Tiepolos, for example – and
they can be easy to confuse.

Among the earlier painters who will catch and
hold the eye are Giovanni Bellini
(c1435–1516), the early Renaissance artist
(see his *Madonna* in the church of the Frari)
and Vittore Carpaccio (c1455–1526), who
gave colour, light and life to paintings
reflecting his own time (see his *St Ursula*
paintings in the Accademia Gallery).

They were followed by the great Titian
(c1485–1576) who added power to the
qualities of the earlier painters (see his *The
Assumption* in the Frari) and Jacopo Tintoretto
(1518–94), who added drama to his Biblical
scenes by the dramatic use of perspective
(see his *Crucifixion* in the Scuola di San
Rocco). In contrast, the paintings of Paolo
Veronese (1528–88) are full of warmth, light
and colour (see his paintings in the church of
San Sabastiano).

In the 18th century, Venice itself came alive in
paintings. Gian Battista Tiepolo (1696–1770)
and his son Gian Domenico Tiepolo
(1727–1804) both reflected the colour and
luxury of Venetian life (see paintings by both
in the Ca'Rezzonico). Pietro Longhi (1702–85)
painted vivid little scenes of everyday
Venetian life (see his series in the
Ca'Rezzonico). Probably the two most popular
painters of Venice itself are Francesco Guardi
(1712–93), who painted slightly
Impressionistic views, and Canaletto
(1697–1768), who painted sharply observed
sunlit scenes and was so popular with English
visitors that he came to London and painted
that city under a sky of Venetian blue (see
work by both in the Accademia Gallery).

Districts and Islands

Venice evolved on islands in a lagoon fed by
rivers and sheltered from the Adriatic by a
barrier of sandbanks. The city itself was built
on a central cluster of islands, divided by two

natural waterways, one of which became the Grand Canal; the other, the Giudecca shipping channel.

To either side of the Grand Canal, the two main masses of the city are divided into six districts, or *sestieri*: San Marco, Cannaregio and Castello to the north and east of the Grand Canal; Dorsoduro, San Polo and Santa Croce to the south and west. The island of Giudecca can be seen as an inner suburb. The other principal islands of the Venetian lagoon lie to the north of the city. Just beyond the cemetery island of San Michele is Murano, which has lived for seven centuries by the manufacture and blowing of glass. Close by is Burano, where the occupations have long been fishing and lace-making. Northward again lies the small agricultural – and now gastronomic – island of Torcello, the first of the Venetian settlements.

Take a break from the city on Burano, a delightful island where fishing boats sail right up to the colourful houses

Also in the northern reaches is, among other small islands, that of San Francesco del Deserto, where part of a 13th-century hermitage survives.

To the southeast of Venice, the seaside resort of the Lido lies along a wide sandbank near one of the three entrances to the lagoon from the open sea. Between the two lie several islands, on one of which, San Lazzaro degli Armeni, an Armenian monastery and centre of learning, can be visited.

Along the sandbanks, reinforced by the great sea-wall, are a number of small settlements and in the extreme south is the town of Chioggia, a major fishing port.

Seen from the air, the city itself – the six *sestieri* to either side of the Grand Canal and the inner island of Giudecca – still looks like a 16th-century artist's idea of how Venice would appear if seen from above.

VENÉZIA-SESTIERI

PONTE DELLA LIBERTA

Canale delle Sacche

Canale delle Navi

Canale delle

CANNAREGIO

Nuova Isola del Tronchetto

Stazione Ferroviaria Santa Lucia

Canal Grande

SANTA CROCE

Porto Commerciale

Bacino della Stazione Marittima

SAN POLO

SAN MARCO

DORSODURO

Canal Grande

Stazione Marittima

Canale di Fusina

Canale della Giudecca

Isola di San Giórgio Maggiore

LA GIUDECCA

0   ½   1 km

WHAT TO SEE IN VENICE (VENÉZIA)

City Layout

Most of Venice may be a maze of canals and alleys but there are particular places where people walk or gather, usually *campi* (squares) or *fondamente* (waterside promenades). The aquatic highway by which they are reached is the main street of the city and that is, of course, the **Grand Canal.**

The Grand Canal

Following the course of an original creek through the muddy islands of the lagoon, the serpentine canal sweeps in two great curves from what is now the Santa Lucia railway station to the Basin of San Marco. It varies in width from 130 to 230 feet (40 to 70m), has a maximum depth of 18 feet (5.5m) and is crossed by three bridges – the Scalzi, the Rialto and the Accademia – and seven *traghetto* (ferry gondola) routes.

Several illustrated guides are devoted solely to the Grand Canal (notably *Canal Grande: Illustrated Tourist Guide* by Lucio Raccanelli; John Kent's *Venice* devotes many pages of illustrations to it) and the better maps will identify the most important buildings.

Travelling eastwards along the Grand Canal, some of the principal buildings between the railway station and the Rialto Bridge are, **on the left bank**, the Scalzi, San Geremia and San Marcuola churches and the palaces Ca'Labia (Tiepolo frescos), Ca' Vendramin-Calergi (the Municipal Casino in winter) and the Ca' d'Oro (museum and art gallery). **On the right bank** are the San Simeone Piccolo and San Stae churches, the palaces Fondaco dei Turchi (Natural History Museum), Ca' Pesaro (Galleries of Modern Art and Oriental Art), Ca' Favretto (Hotel San Cassiano) – and then the fish, fruit and vegetable markets just before the Rialto Bridge.

Between the Rialto and the Accademia bridges are, **on**

Murano

Isola di San Michele

Fondamenta Nuove

Bacini di Carenággio

Dársena Grande

Isola di San Pietro

CASTELLO

Dársena di Sant' Elena

Canale di San Marco

Isola di Sant' Elena

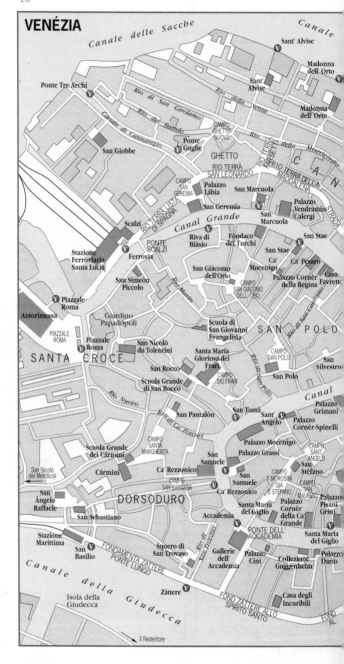

VENÉZIA

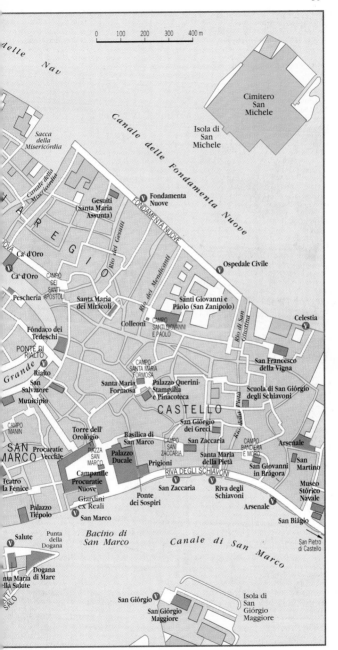

Check your watch with the Torre dell' Orologio in Piazza S Marco

the left bank, the church of San Samuele and the Ca' Mocenigo (where Lord Byron began to write *Don Juan*; not to be confused with the Palazzo Mocenigo which is open to the public) and Ca' Grassi (exhibitions centre); **on the right bank**, the palace, Ca' Rezzonico (museum of 18th-century arts) – then, at the Accademia Bridge, the Accademia Gallery in the former church and *scuola* of Santa Maria della Carità. Between the Accademia Bridge and the Basin of San Marco are, **on the left bank**. Ca' Barbaro (where many artists and writers stayed and Henry James wrote *The Aspern Papers*); Ca' Grande (Prefecture of Police); Ca' Pisani-Gritti (Gritti Palace Hotel); Ca' Tiepolo (Europa e Regina Hotel) – and then the buildings around the Piazza San Marco.

Piazza San Marco

The Piazza San Marco is the heart of Venice. When Napoleon conquered the Venetian Republic he called it 'the most elegant drawing-room in Europe', and so it still is. At the eastern end stands the Basilica di San Marco with its Byzantine domes; to one side its campanile, the Piazzetta outside the Doges' Palace and the Basin of San Marco; to the other the Clock Tower and the Piazzetta dei Leoncini, named after the red marble lions standing there. The north side of the Piazza is bounded by the **Procuratie Vecchie**, the former offices of the Republic's administration, with an arcade of shops below and the Café Quadri, once patronised by the Austrian occupiers of Venice. On the south side are the former administration building, the **Procuratie Nuove** with another arcade of shops and the Café Florian, the favourite of Venetian patriots during the Austrian occupation, below. At the western end of the Piazza, the church of San Geminiano was demolished on Napoleon's orders and a new arcade with a ballroom above was built (the entrance of the Correr Museum of Venetian history is now there, see page 55). The two granite columns near the water's edge in the Piazzetta were set up in the 12th century; one is surmounted by a stone Lion of St Mark, the other by the figure of St Theodore, the first patron saint of the city, proudly wielding shield and spear.

On the right bank are the church of Santa Maria della Salute and the palaces of Ca' Venier dei Leoni (the unfinished palace housing the Peggy Guggenheim Collection of Modern Art), Ca' Dario (its façade richly inlaid with multi-coloured marble) and, at the extreme end, the Dogana di Mare (the Customs House), viewable from outside only. The whole length of the Grand Canal is covered by the Nos 1 and 4 *vaporetto* routes.

CITY LAYOUT

Promenades and Squares
The **Riva degli Shiavoni** (The Waterfront of the Slavs) is the principal waterside promenade of Venice, running eastwards from the Doges' Palace to the Ca' di Dio canal, where its name changes; then continuing to the Giardini (public gardens). After the Doges' Palace and the adjoining State Prison comes the Hotel Danieli and a succession of other grand hotels (see pages 90-2) facing the Basin of San Marco. The wide, paved Riva, broken by a succession of bridges over canals, is cluttered with café tables and souvenir-sellers'

An original from the artists along Riva degli Schiavoni is an attractive Venetian souvenir

stalls at its western end, while its waterside is busy with *vaporetto* piers and the pleasure boats and tugs that moor there.

Leading from the Riva to the north are many alleys and archways running into the maze of the city and to a few squares, notably the Campo San Zaccaria and the Campo Bandera e Moro. Beyond the canal leading to the Arsenale, lie the Giardini, the public gardens, rather dusty and unkempt but with fine tall trees, among which are the pavilions where the Biennale art exhibition is held. This rare open space is where Napoleon demolished the buildings to lay out defensive batteries.

There are two churches, the **Pietà** and the rarely-opened **San Biagio**, near the Naval Museum, along the Riva. The **Fondamenta delle Zattere** is the second most popular waterside promenade, stretching from the docks and the maritime station to the Dogana along the southern shore of the Dorsoduro district and facing across the wide Giudecca Canal to Giudecca island. There are three churches on the Zattere: **Santa Maria della Visitazione**, the **Gesuati** and the **Spirito Santo**. There is also a succession of inexpensive restaurants and two of the smaller hotels (see pages 78, 93 and 95).

The **Ghetto** – a small district enclosed by canals in the northwest of the city and not far from the railway station – was the first Jewish enclave of

that name (its name derived from that of the cannon-casting foundry which was there in the 14th century) and remains a centre for that religion. Since Jews were only permitted to live in this small area from 1516 to 1797, they were allowed to build higher houses than elsewhere in the city and these rise to eight storeys. There are still a number of Jewish families living in the three sections of the Ghetto, as well as synagogues and shops selling Jewish books and souvenirs. In the principal *campo*, a memorial commemorates the Holocaust. *Vaporetto*: San Marcuola.
Throughout the city, *campi*, or squares, are meeting-places and markets for Venetians, often including a parish church, cafés and shops. On the San Marco side of the Grand Canal, they include the **Campo Santi Giovanni e Paolo**, outside the huge church of San Zanipolo (see page 32), which is dominated by the remarkable equestrian bronze statue of **Bartolomeo Colleoni**, a famous Venetian general of the 15th century. A short walk to the south is the **Campo Santa Maria Formosa** around the church of that name (see page 42), busy with market stalls and open-air café tables. On the other side of the Grand Canal, the largest is **Campo San Polo**, where the huge marble well-head is a gathering-place for the young on summer evenings. More lively is the **Campo Santa Margherita**, where stalls sell fruit, vegetables, fish and shoes

The statue of Carlo Goldini stands watch over the church of San Bartolomeo

and local Venetian life goes on undisturbed by crowds of tourists.
Perhaps the most charmingly Venetian of all the squares is the **Campo San Barnaba** near the Accademia Gallery (*vaporetto*: Ca'Rezzonico). Presided over by the noble façade of the church of San Barnaba (a simple parish church with an air of tranquillity) this bustles with life: shops, two cafés with tables outside and a barge selling vegetables and fruit moored in the canal that connects with the Grand Canal.

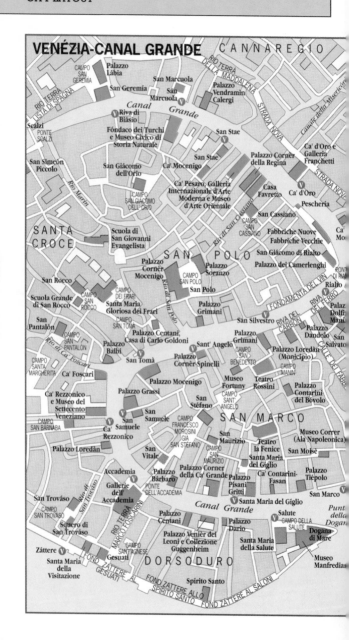

Palaces
Few of the scores of Venetian palaces are open to the public and those privately owned are often shuttered and empty, or split into flats. For an idea of their interiors, take a *vaporetto* along the Canal Grande after dark and look up at the lighted windows and you may glimpse paintings in gilded frames, tapestries, frescos, painted ceilings and chandeliers of Murano glass.

Those palaces that are open to the public are nearly all museums or hotels and are much altered inside. The *palazzi* that are now museums include the **Ca' d'Oro** (Italian art), **Ca' Pesaro** (modern and Oriental art), **Ca' Rezzonico** (the 18th century), **Centani** (dedicated to the playwright Goldoni), **Fondaco dei Turchi** (natural history), **Mocenigo** (textiles), **Pesaro degli Orfei** (Fortuny), **Querini-Stampalia** (arts) and **Venier dei Leoni** (Guggenheim) – see **Museums**, pages 50-7.

There is one palace which every visitor to Venice must see.

◆◆◆
PALAZZO DUCALE (THE DOGES' PALACE) ✓

Piazzetta di San Marco
Venice was governed from the Doges' Palace for a thousand years and it still dominates the city. The pink palace with its white colonnades that we see across the water from the Basin of San Marco, looks much as it did when it replaced an earlier building in the 14th century,

PALACES

Arrive early when it's quieter to enjoy the Palazzo Ducale

except that its pillars seem foreshortened because the level of the surrounding pavement has been raised. Here the elected Doge, or Duke, of Venice held his court (see **History**, pages 8-11) and presided over a system of councils, designed to prevent any one self-interested faction seizing power. Once, when this failed, the over-ambitious Doge Marin Falier was convicted of treason and beheaded at the top of the new marble staircase in the palace courtyard and his portrait replaced by a black cloth, which can still be seen. Visitors to the palace can marvel at the succession of richly-decorated council chambers on the second floor, their walls and ceilings painted by the leading Venetian painters, including Tintoretto's *Paradise*, the largest Old Master painting in the world. That is on the wall of the Sala del Maggior Consiglio (Great Council Chamber), a vast hall designed to seat 1,700 citizens who had the right to vote in the council.

serving a five-year sentence on charges involving blasphemy, magic and espionage.

The Doges' Palace is so rich in art and architectural splendours that a whole morning or afternoon could be devoted to it. When Venice is crowded, it is best to arrive early to enjoy an unhurried tour.

Open: daily 09.00 to 19.00 hours, closing earlier in winter. Tours of the 'secret rooms' (*itinerari segreti*) leave the main entrance at stated times, currently twice a day except Sunday, and must be booked at least a day in advance (for more information about these telephone 5224951).

Vaporetto: San Marco or San Zaccaria.

Other Palaces

The **Palazzo Grassi**, San Marco 3231, Campo San Samuele (tel: 5235133), on the Grand Canal, is used for temporary art exhibitions and antiques fairs. It is a vast 18th-century palace with notable frescos but was much modernised in the 1980s for its pressent use.

The **Palazzo Labia**, on the Campo San Geremia and the Fondamenta San Giobbe (not far from the Santa Lucia railway station) is now the headquarters of the Italian broadcasting service, RAI. But it contains one of the loveliest rooms in Venice decorated by the elder Tiepolo with gloriously-coloured frescos of Anthony and Cleopatra in 18th-century dress and dramatic

From the Palace itself, the **Ponte dei Sospiri** (Bridge of Sighs) crosses a canal to the prison and the dungeons below water-level known as 'the wells' (*pozzi*). Visitors may join guided tours through the Palace and the prison and also special tours of the 'secret rooms' (led by a guide who speaks only Italian). This includes the interrogation rooms and torture chamber of the State Inquisitors and the cells under the roof of the prison, called 'the leads', from which Casanova made his dramatic escape in 1756, while

PALACES

perspectives.
Open: by appointment 15.00 to 16.00 hours Wednesday, Thursday and Friday. Arrangements to view can be made by hotel staff (tel: 716666).
Vaporetto: Ferrovia.
One that can only be seen from outside is the **Palazzo Contarini**, which has a remarkable spiral staircase in its open courtyard on the Calle della Vida, close to the Compo Manin. The Bovolo Staircase,

as it is called (*bovolo* means spiral in Venetian dialect), is a remarkably delicate feat of architecture and is best seen by moonlight.
Vaporetto: Rialto or Sant' Angelo.
Many of the larger hotels were once palaces and some retain a few of their original internal features. The office of the British Consulate at the Dorsoduro end of the Accademia Bridge is in one of the smaller palaces and is reached by a marble staircase decorated with *trompe-l'oeil* frescos.

The remarkable Bovolo Staircase of the Palazzo Contarini

Churches

Churches are among the greatest splendours of Venice. They may be magnificently simple in design, with white and grey marble expressing baroque beauty or Palladian dignity. Or they may be small, dark and glitteringly ornate, like the inside of a jewel-box, whether they date from the Renaissance or the decadent 18th century.

They may be seen as the centrepiece of some great vista across water, or lie hidden in some teeming alley or deserted *campo*.

Church-visiting should be concentrated in the morning, when they are most likely to be open. Although churches are supposed to be open before noon and from late afternoon until early evening, they are often closed and some seem to be permanently locked. Usually, however, a notice by the door will give the times of opening and the times of Sunday services (on Sundays it is best to see the church immediately before or after the service to avoid interruption; otherwise, if a service is in progress, it is courteous to stand silently just inside the entrance without wandering about). Where possible, specific times of opening are given in the individual entries, and also, where applicable, the nearest *vaporetto* to the church.

Dedicated church-visitors joke that trying to find the more obscure churches open can be as exciting as stalking rare birds is to ornithologists.

A detail from the exquisite mosaics in Basilica di S Marco

Essential Viewing

◆◆◆
BASILICA DI SAN MARCO (ST MARK'S BASILICA) ✓

Piazza San Marco
The cathedral of Venice evokes the blending of East and West that is at the heart of the Venetian character. More oriental than European, the architecture, the decoration and the atmosphere of ancient sanctity span both the centuries and the styles of Mediterranean civilisation. Originally built to house the body of St Mark, the patron saint of Venice, which had been smuggled from its tomb in Alexandria by Venetians in AD 828, the

basilica evolved its present appearance between the 9th and 19th centuries. The basic building dates from the late 11th century, the domes from the 13th and the decoration from subsequent centuries. Much of the decoration was plundered or presented to Venice during its time of supremacy, most notably the four famous gilded horses above the main doors. Made in the 4th century AD to surmount a Roman truimphal arch, they were looted from Constantinople, when it was sacked by the Venetians during the Crusades, and stood on the façade for nearly 600 years until plundered, in turn, by the French. After the Napoleonic wars, they were restored to the basilica although, because of atmospheric pollution, the originals are now kept in a gallery inside while replicas stand in their place.

The richness of ornament outside and inside the basilica can occupy hours but even the hurried visitor can admire the glowing gold of the mosaics which cover an acre of the vaulting, or examine them more closely from the galleries. The most famous single treasure of San Marco is the elaborate gold Byzantine altarpiece, the *Pala d'Oro*. Started in the 10th century, it was not completed until 1342. To see this and the treasury there is an entrance charge. *Open:* daily 09.45 to 18.30 hours.

Pala d'Oro and Treasury closed Sunday morning.

Basilica S Marco makes a splendid setting for a leisurely espresso

◆◆◆
CAMPANILE DI SAN MARCO (ST MARK'S BELL TOWER)

The tower rises 325 feet (99m) above the piazza, the tallest building in Venice. The original collapsed in 1902 but was rebuilt over the next 10 years. It is entered through the beautiful little *loggetta,* built in the 16th century by Jacopo Sansovino and restored after it was destroyed by the

collapsing campanile. A lift takes visitors to the gallery surrounding the belfry, which commands panoramic views of the city, the lagoon and, on clear days, the Veneto and the Alps.
Open: daily, 10.00 to 19.00 hours.
Entrance charge.

The basilica has been the cathedral of Venice only since 1807. Before that time it had been the shrine of San Marco and the chapel of the Doge, while the church of San Pietro di Castello in the far east of the city (see page 44) had been the cathedral, an arrangement to minimise the influence of the Papacy on the affairs of Venice.

There are two other churches, much larger than either of these, one to either side of the Grand Canal. The survival of both colossal buildings bears testimony to the strength of the medieval foundations of the city laid in the mud of the lagoon islands.

◆◆◆
SANTI GIOVANNI E PAOLO
(ST JOHN AND ST PAUL)
Campo Santi Giovanni e Paolo, Castello

Called San Zanipolo by Venetians, the church stands to the north of San Marco. The largest church in Venice, it was built by the Dominicans in the 14th and 15th centuries. Despite its bulk, the red brick building is not ponderous, partly because of the recent cleaning of the elaborate Gothic portals at the west end and the monuments within. Inside, the original choir screen and stalls have not survived, leaving the nave light and airy. Around the walls stand magnificent monuments to Doges and, amongst other notables, the Venetian general, Marcantonio Bragadin, who was flayed alive by the Turks when they captured Cyprus in 1571. Not only does a fresco on the monument depict this, but the flayed skin, which was stolen from Constantinople, lies in a small sarcophagus. His death was swiftly avenged at the Battle of Lepanto by the Doge Sebastiano Venier, whose fine bronze statue also stands in the church.

Open: 07.30 to 12.30 and 15.30 to 19.30 hours

Red brick Basilica SS Giovanni e Paolo, the city's largest church

◆◆◆
SANTA MARIA GLORIOSA DEI FRARI (THE FRARI) ✓

Campo Dei Frari, San Polo
This church stands on the far side of the Canal Grande. It is almost as large as Santi Giovanni e Paolo but has a wholly different character. The choir screen and stalls remain in place and the nave is shadowed and sombre, as are the vast and elaborate monuments. Memorable among these is the open - doored pyramid containing the heart of the 18th-century sculptor Antonio Canova. He designed it as a monument to the great Venetian painter Titian, who, in fact, is buried across the aisle under a dramatic 19th-century statue.

Two paintings are the particular glories of the Frari. One is Titian's huge *The Assumption*, still in the position for which it was painted above the high altar. The other is *The Madonna and Child* by Bellini in the sacristy, one of the loveliest paintings in Venice.

Like San Zanipolo (see previous page), the Frari can easily occupy an hour or more for those with a particular interest in painting, sculpture and architecture.
Open: 09.00 to 12.00 and 14.30 to 18.00 hours Monday to Saturday;
15.00 to 17.30 hours, Sunday (slightly reduced hours in winter).
Entrance charge.
Vaporetto: San Toma.

Other Churches
A selection of churches is listed alphabetically below. They are related to any nearby reference points and *sestieri*, or districts for easy location. There are six *sestieri:* to the north and east of the Grand Canal, San Marco is in the centre, Castello to the east and Cannaregio to the west; to the south and west, Dorsoduro lies across the Grand Canal from San Marco with San Polo, then Santa Croce, to the north (see map, pages 16-17).

◆
ANGELO RAFFAELE
Dorsoduro
This is a large church in need of restoration in a poor district towards the docks, but notable for its 18th-century organ decorated with charming paintings by Guardi.

◆
CARMINI (SANTA MARIA DEL CARMELO)
Dorsoduro
Near the Campo Santa Margherita, this is a large, sombre church displaying many paintings, including a series in the nave illustrating the history of the Carmelite Order.

◆
GESUATI (SANTA MARIA DEL ROSARIO)
Fondamenta del Zattere, Dorsoduro
This is a surprisingly large church, its white and grey stone interior enlivened by the colour and zest of ceiling and altar paintings by Tiepolo.
Vaporetto: Zattere.

The 'silk' drapes of Gesuiti are in reality made of marble

◆◆
GESUITI (SANTA MARIA ASSUNTA)

near the Fondamenta Nuove, Cannaregio

Not to be confused with the Gesuati, this is also near ships and open water. The early 18th-century Jesuits built their church to impress, and the statuary along the skyline of its pediment gives a hint of what is within. There, the pillars and floor seem to be hung with green and white damask silk, which is also draped and ruffled around the pulpit on the north wall; but it all turns out to be marble.

Vaporetto: Fondamenta Nuove.

◆
GIGLIO (SANTA MARIA DEL GIGLIO)

on the route between San Marco and the Accademia Bridge
This appears the most worldly church in Venice, because the carvings on its façade depict fortified cities and warships. These commemorate the naval and diplomatic career of Antonio Barbaro, whose family paid for the building of the façade as his monument.
Vaporetto: Santa Maria del Giglio.

◆◆
MADONNA DELL' ORTO

Cannaregio
Isolated in the north of the city, the church is a good goal for a long walk. A huge, light, airy church reminiscent of San Zanipolo, it was magnificently restored after the flood of 1966 by funds raised in Britain. Tintoretto, who is buried in one of the side chapels, was a parishioner and painted a number of pictures for the church, including the enormous *The Last Judgement* and *The Adoration of the Golden Calf,* both in the chancel, two paintings behind the high altar and the charming *The Presentation of the Virgin.*
Vaporetto: Madonna dell' Orto.

◆◆◆
MIRACOLI (SANTA MARIA DEI MIRACOLI)✓

Campo dei Miracoli, Cannaregio
One of the most exquisite small buildings in Venice, this church has often been described as looking like a jewel-box. Built in the 15th century of softly-coloured marble, it stands beside a canal with such elegance that its design needs no embellishment to satisfy the eye. When closed, the outer doors are often left open so that the interior, which is as lovely as the exterior, can be admired through an inner glass door.

◆
OSPEDALETTO (SANTA MARIA DEI DERELITTI)

near San Zanipolo, Castello
This is one of the Venetian oddities. Built in the late 17th century, its façade is a sculptured riot of grotesque figures and its interior is cluttered with ornament and paintings of the 17th and 18th centuries.

◆
PIETÀ

Riva degli Schiavoni, San Marco
This has been used for concerts since the 17th century, and during the 18th century Vivaldi composed music for the choir. Music is still played here regularly on Monday evenings, when audiences can take the opportunity to admire the oval painting by Tiepolo in the ceiling, *The Coronation of the Virgin.* The church is usually closed from Tuesday to Thursday.
Vaporetto: Riva Schiavoni

◆
REDENTORE

Giudecca island
This is best seen across the water from the centre of Venice. Indeed, its architect, Palladio, who was commissioned to design it as an

CHURCHES

act of thanksgiving for the ending of a 16th-century plague, intended it to catch and hold the distant eye. The façade and the interior together form a magnificent example of what came to be known as Palladian architecture. On the third Sunday of July, a bridge of boats is constructed across the Giudecca Canal for the celebration of the Feast of the Redentore. The church is dramatically floodlit at night. *Vaporetto:* Redentore.

♦♦♦
SALUTE (SANTA MARIA DELLA SALUTE) ✓

Dorsoduro, near the eastern end of the Grand Canal
Like the Redentore this church was built to give thanks for the ending of a plague, but in the following century. The great domed church at the entrance to the Grand Canal has sometimes been seen as the hostess of the city, welcoming visitors; as the novelist Henry James wrote: 'like some great lady on the threshold of her salon … with her domes and scrolls, her scalloped buttresses and statues forming a pompous crown, and her wide steps disposed on the ground like the train of a robe.' After dark, a walk through the alleys of Dorsoduro can suddenly end on the brilliantly floodlit steps of the Salute beneath its gleaming bulk, the water below dancing with reflected light.
The magnificent baroque interior is decorated with

paintings by Titian.
Vaporetto: Salute

♦
SANT' ALVISE

Campo Sant' Alvise, Cannaregio
Although one of the most remote (and often shut) churches in the city, this is a useful destination for a long walk including the Madonna dell' Orto and the Ghetto (see

Salute at sunset, seen from the island of S Giorgio Maggiore

pages 35 and 22). Its most notable painting (by Tiepolo) having been removed to the Accademia Gallery, its principle feature is now a spectacular but clumsily-executed painted ceiling. This depicts Heaven as seen from a grandiose courtyard shown in architectural perspectives painted on the flat surface and is a cruder version of the extraordinary painted ceiling in San Pantalon (see page 43).
Vaporetto: Sant' Alvise.

◆
SANTI APOSTOLI
Cannaregio
The ceiling painting here is a rather more sophisticated version of *The Righteous Ascending to Heaven* than that in Sant' Alvise (see above). The church is worth visiting for the lovely painting, *The Communion of Santa Lucia* by the elder Tiepolo and the 15th-century Corner family chapel. There is an exceptionally tall 17th-century campanile.
Vaporetto: Ca' d'Oro.

CHURCHES

◆
SAN CASSIANO
Campo San Cassiano, San Polo
This sumptuous church, with its pillars draped in crimson, is worth visiting for Tintoretto's majestic *Crucifixion*.
Vaporetto: San Stae.

◆
SAN FRANCESCO DELLA VIGNA
Campo della Confraternità, Castello
This is a large church in the less-visited northeast of the city near the Arsenale, and its huge campanile is sometimes mistaken for that of San Marco from a distance. It contains beautiful paintings – although none of the first rank – including a delightful *Madonna and Child Enthroned* by Antonio da Negroponte.
Vaporetto: Arsenale.

◆
SAN GEREMIA
Cannaregio
Standing on the corner of the Grand Canal and the Canale di Cannaregio, this vast, light, plain church is now remarkable for housing the body of Santa Lucia, which was removed from her own church when it was demolished to make way for the railway station that was to be named after her. Wearing a gold mask and a red and gold robe, she lies in a glass case.
Vaporetto: Ferrovia.

◆◆
SAN GIACOMO DELL' ORIO
Santa Croce
A busy parish church in a quiet *campo* in the northwest of the

city, where the only visitors are likely to be those walking to the Piazzale Roma to catch a bus. Its styles of architecture and decoration reflect the growth of Venice: pillars from Byzantium and one of the two 'ship's keel' roofs (like an inverted wooden ship) in Venice – the other is in Santo Stefano; paintings by Venetian masters, including Veronese; and, in comic contrast, a funny little relief carving of a knight – almost a cartoon character – on the outside wall.
Vaporetto: San Stae.

◆
SAN GIACOMO DI RIALTO
Campo San Giacomo, San Polo
It stands among the fruit and vegetable market stalls at the foot of the Rialto Bridge. The oldest church in the city – said to have been founded in the early 5th century – it has grown many architectural and decorative curiosities, including a rare brick dome, over-large baroque altarpieces and, most notably, a large, blue 15th-century clock on the façade. It faces the market square, which was once used by Venetian bankers, money-changers and insurance brokers – including, presumably, Shakespeare's Shylock.
Vaporetto: Rialto.

◆
SAN GIOBBE
Campo San Giobbe, Cannaregio
Another remote church to the northwest of the city, it is often locked. Suffering from damp and in need of restoration, it is worth a visit to see those of its

After the daily fruit and vegetable
market outside S Giacomo di Rialto
– the oldest church in Venice

paintings that have not been
removed to the Accademia
Gallery, including a triptych by
Antonio Vivarini.

◆
SAN GIORGIO DEI GRECI
Castello
The church is quickly
recognisable by its
dangerously tilted 16th-century
campanile. The church of the
Greek community – many of

whom were refugees from
Constantinople when it was
taken by the Turks in the 15th
century – its decoration is
strongly Byzantine and Greek
Orthodox.
Vaporetto: San Zaccaria.

◆◆◆
SAN GIORGIO MAGGIORE
Isola San Giorgio Maggiore
The church stands on its island
across the Basin of San Marco,
giving Venice one of its most
celebrated views. Designed by
Andrea Palladio in the 16th
century, it has all the majesty

Don't miss a trip to the celebrated island of S Giorgio Maggiore – and the view from the church tower into its peaceful cloister

that the term 'Palladian' implies and this is particularly apparent at night when the façade is floodlit. The interior is vast and austere, its white stone a magnificent setting for its works of art, including paintings by Tintoretto and a bronze altarpiece, *The Globe Surmounted by God the Father,* dating from the 16th century.

The tall campanile, ascended by a lift, offers the best such view of Venice because, unlike that of San Marco, it is detached from the city which can therefore be seen as a panorama across the water. *Vaporetto:* San Giorgio.

◆◆
SAN GIOVANNI IN BRAGORA
Campo Bandiera e Moro, Castello
A fascinating little parish church, where Vivaldi was once the organist, it lies hidden in a quiet *campo* off the Riva

◆◆
SAN GIULIANO
Campo San Zulian, San Marco
Known by Venetians as San
Zulian, it is in the midst of busy
shopping alleys, just north of the
Piazza San Marco.
Although its exterior is in need of
the restoration which is probably
to be funded by the British
branch of the Venice in Peril
Fund, the interior is opulent and
very Venetian. Golden cherubs
hold a draped red backcloth
behind the gilded and richly
decorated high altar, and the
ceiling is painted with the
familiar and spectacular Venetian
view of heaven from earth.

SANTA MARIA ASSUNTA *see*
GESUITI

SANTA MARIA DEL
CARMELO *see* CARMINI

SANTA MARIA DEI DERELITTI
see OSPEDALETTO

◆
SANTA MARIA DELLA FAVA
*Campo Santa Maria della Fava,
San Marco*
This is a high-ceilinged church
decorated by much grey
statuary by Bernardi, the teacher
of Canova, and a beautiful early
painting by Tiepolo, *The
Education of the Virgin.*
Vaporetto: Rialto.

SANTA MARIA DEL GIGLIO *see*
GIGLIO

SANTA MARIA DEI MIRACOLI
see MIRACOLI

SANTA MARIA DI NAZARETH
see SCALZI

degli Schiavoni. Among its
paintings is a lovely, peaceful
Madonna by Bartolomeo
Vivarini.
Vaporetto: Arsenale.

◆
SAN GIOVANNI
CRISOSTOMO
*Campo San Giovanni
Crisostomo, Cannaregio*
A small, busy, very Venetian
parish church. Richly
decorated, it is remarkable for
a lovely painting of saints by
Giovanni Bellini.
Vaporetto: Rialto.

CHURCHES

*The vast, cool interior of Palladio's
S Giorgio Maggiore*

SANTA MARIA DEL ROSARIO
see **GESUATI**

SANTA MARIA DELLA
SALUTE *see* **SALUTE**

◆
SANTA MARIA FORMOSA
*Campo Santa Maria Formosa,
Castello*
The 15th-century church
dominates a large square
enlivened by cafés and market
stalls. It is filled with interesting
monuments and paintings,
including works by Vivarini
(*The Madonna of Mercy*) and
Palma il Vecchio (*The
Martyrdom of St Barbara*).
Outside, at the base of the
campanile, is the carved stone
mask of a bearded man

'leering in brutal degradation',
as described by the art
historian John Ruskin, who
could hardly bring himself to
look at it.

◆◆
SAN MARTINO
Castello
This is a lovely, little-visited
church near the Arsenale, and it
is probable that the wooden
angels and cherubs around the
organ were carved by
craftsmen who decorated the
great galleys in the dockyard. It
has another spectacular ceiling
painted with an *Ascension into
Heaven*, past the pillars of an
atrium, that seems to grow out
of the architecture. The
profusion of monuments and
paintings makes this another
very Venetian church, and

outside in the wall is one of the now-rare 'lion's mask' letterboxes for notes denouncing enemies of the state.
Vaporetto: Arsenale.

SAN MAURIZIO
Campo San Maurizio, San Marco
This faces the square on the route between San Marco and the Accademia Bridge, where antiques markets are occasionally held. Originally an ancient church, it was completely rebuilt in 1806 when Venice was under French rule and so is often ignored by admirers of the Venetian Republic. It is a handsome, plain church in neoclassical style, its cool and elegant interior given a dramatic focal point by the white marble tabernacle on the high altar, thrown into relief by the red drapery behind, held by gilded cherubs above.

◆
SAN MOISÈ
Campo San Moisè, San Marco
The church, with its over-elaborate façade, now much in need of cleaning, commands the view of those walking towards San Marco from the Accademia bridge. Its interior is just as odd: the high altar appears at first sight to be a bizarre rockery but turns out to be a tableau of *Moses on Mount Sinai Receiving the Tablets*. The building is in startling contrast to the smooth, smart looks of the Hotel Bauer Grünwald next door.
Vaporetto: San Marco.

SAN NICOLÒ DEI MENDICOLI
Campo San Nicolò, Dorsoduro
The parish church of a poor district of the city near the docks, it is both modest and ornate. Restored by British contributions to the Venice in Peril Fund in 1977, its gilded wooden statues gleam anew. Built between the 12th and 15th centuries and well-stocked with statuary and paintings, it is a good goal when exploring the hinterland of the western end of the Zattere and visiting the nearby churches of San Sebastiano and Angelo Raffaele.
Vaporetto: San Basilio.

◆
SAN NICOLÒ DA TOLENTINI
Campo dei Tolentini, Santa Croce
This colossal church with a vast, pillared Corinthian portico is close to the Piazzale Roma and the car parks and so popular for weddings. Inside, it is elaborate, enriched with sculpture and paintings, and has a 'whispering gallery' around the inside rim of its dome.
Vaporetto: Piazzale Roma.

SAN PANTALÒN
Campo San Pantalòn, Dorsoduro
This probably makes a more immediate impact on the visitor than any church in Venice. On entering and looking up, the vast flat ceiling can be seen to be one enormous view of a mass ascent into Heaven. This startling scene also includes

CHURCHES

the life and martyrdom of San Pantalòn and was painted at the end of the 17th century and the beginning of the 18th. A typically quirky Venetian postscript is the fate of the artist, Gian Antonio Fumiani, who, as he completed his work, stepped back to admire it better, fell from the scaffolding to his death and was buried in the church he had decorated so memorably. The church also contains smaller works by Veronese and Vivarini. Like several other Venetian churches, it has no façade as its builders ran out of money.

SAN PIETRO DI CASTELLO
Isola di San Pietro
As it stands forlornly on its little island at the far eastern extremity of Venice, the church seems to be dreaming of past glories. This was the first of the central Venetian islands to be settled, and the church became the cathedral of Venice in AD 775, remaining so until 1807, when that dignity was bestowed upon the Basilica di San Marco, formerly the Doges' private chapel. Its isolation here throughout the life of the Venetian Republic was a deliberate attempt to minimise the influence of the Pope and Rome. It overlooks a usually deserted stretch of grass and trees. Inside, the church, which was built to replace its predecessors in the 16th and 17th centuries, is lofty and rather grand but, above all, sad.
Vaporetto: Giardini.

SAN POLO
Campo San Polo, San Polo
The church stands in the largest square in the city after San Marco. Its works of art include fine bronze statues of saints on the high altar and paintings by both Tiepolos with 14 paintings of *The Stations of the Cross* by the younger.
Vaporetto: San Toma.

SAN ROCCO
Campo San Rocco, San Polo
Standing beside the famous *scuola* (see page 49), it is chiefly remarkable for large paintings of the saint's miracles by Tintoretto.

SAN SALVATORE
Campo San Salvador, San Marco
Now under long-term restoration this is regarded as one of the finest Renaissance churches in Italy. Principally admired for its architecture, its works of art include a painting by Titian of *The Annunciation*.
Vaporetto: Rialto.

SAN SEBASTIANO
Campo San Sebastiano, Dorsoduro
The most important of the three major churches near the docks, it belongs to the great painter Paolo Veronese, who decorated it and is buried there. His works are everywhere in the church, including the open doors of the organ and the ceiling, in the chancel, the sacristy and the gallery, where he painted frescos on the walls. In all, he painted here the richest and

most comprehensive exhibition of his own work and one that no admirer of Venetian art should miss. Sadly, opening times of the church are unpredictable and it has recently been closed for long-term restoration. Check with the tourist office as to its opening times.
Vaporetto: San Basilio.

◆◆
SAN STAE
Canal Grande, Santa Croce
This is a church that is best seen from outside, handsome as its interior is. Its neoclassical façade, decorated with joyous baroque statuary, provides one of the most striking views on the Grand Canal. Sadly, however, the beautiful little goldsmiths' *scuola* that adjoins it – one of the prettiest

buildings in Venice – is now empty and near-derelict. The church itself is used for art exhibitions.
Vaporetto: San Stae.

◆◆
SANTO STEFANO
Campo Francesco Morosini, San Marco
A large, handsome church with one of the two 'ship's keel' roofs – like a huge, inverted wooden hull – in the city (the other is in San Giacomo dell'Orio). Richly painted and decorated with inlaid, multi-coloured marble, it contains paintings by Tintoretto. Outside are cloisters and a leaning 16th-century campanile.

◆
SAN TROVASO
Campo San Trovaso, Dorsoduro
This is a huge Palladian church with two identical façades

S Zaccaria displays fine paintings

because, it is said, two rival
16th-century families each
wanted to be the first to enter
and so could do so
simultaneously. The interior is
lofty, light and peaceful;
outside, the *campo* in front of
the two main doors is a good
place to sit in the sun away
from the city bustle.
Vaporetto: Zattere.

◆◆◆
SAN ZACCARIA
Campo San Zaccaria, Castello
The massive 16th-century
church – with traces of its
predecessors – is filled with
paintings. The most celebrated
of these is Bellini's *Madonna
and Child* in the north aisle
(restored in 1976). During the
Venetian Republic, the nunnery
attached to the church was
favoured by rich families as a
refuge for their unattached
daughters. There is also a
flooded crypt where several
Doges are interred (entrance
charge).
Vaporetto: San Zaccaria.

◆◆
SCALZI (SANTA MARIA DI NAZARETH)
Fondamenta Scalzi Cannaregio
Close to the railway station, the
church is well-placed for those
wanting a first, or last, look at
something intensely Venetian.
The ornate baroque façade is
an indication of the sumptuous
gloom within, all multi-coloured
marble, statuary and 18th-
century paintings dimly seen,
and a high altar with twisted
marble columns. Suitably, the
last of the Doges, Ludovico
Manin, is buried there.
Vaporetto: Ferrovia.

*The entrance to the Arsenale –
where the great ships of the
Venetian Empire were built and
berthed*

Landmarks
Many of the most celebrated
buildings in Venice are neither
churches nor palaces but those
built for a specific purpose in
the life of the city.

◆
ARSENALE
The naval power-house of the
Venetian Empire was the
Arsenale, the great dockyard in

the east of the city. Surrounded by 15th-century castellated walls and entered through a monumental archway and watergate, it was where the galleys that conquered the Mediterranean and dominated it for centuries were built and based. The interior is now mostly deserted dockside and bare walls, but the gates – guarded by stone lions brought from Greece in the 17th and 18th centuries – can be admired from the *campiello* outside. The No 5 *vaporetto* – the *circolare* – passes through the *Arsenale,* between the flanking towers of the entrance and an arch in the north walls.

◆◆◆

DOGANA DI MARE (CUSTOMS HOUSE)

This stands where the Dorsoduro district of Venice to the east of the church of the Salute just like a ship's prow into the lagoon at the junction of the Canal Grande and the Basin of San Marco. On top of its tower stand two bronze figures of Atlas holding up a golden globe surmounted by a figure of Fortune as a wind-vane. Behind the tower are the 17th-century Customs warehouses. Not open to the public except for exhibitions.

◆◆◆
PONTE DI RIALTO (RIALTO BRIDGE)✔

Built of Istrian stone in the late 16th century this was, until 1854, the only crossing of the Grand Canal and replaced a wooden bridge. A single span, decorated with relief carvings and balustrades, it is famous for its parallel rows of shops facing one another to either side of the central path. These sell mostly jewellery, leather goods, silk

Shoes for the well-heeled are for sale on the Ponte di Rialto

and shoes. The bridge commands fine views of the Grand Canal, particularly in the direction of San Marco.

◆◆◆
SQUERO DI SAN TROVASO
on the San Trovaso Canal near the Zattere
This is a picturesque boatyard where gondolas have been built and repaired for hundreds of years. It is a favourite subject for photographs taken, with the church of San Trovaso in the background, from the other side of the canal.
Not open to the public.

◆◆◆
TEATRO LA FENICE
Campo San Fantin, San Marco
The opera house of Venice is as remarkable for its interior as for any performance. Built in the

late 18th century and rebuilt after a fire in the early 19th, it is one of the oldest and most beautiful theatres in Europe. Behind the severe façade, the gilded auditorium is a blaze of light and colour. Although the opera season is in winter, the theatre is usually open for concerts and recitals throughout the year except in August, when the theatre is closed. The auditorium is best seen from the upper galleries, and there is the added advantage that the seats are cheaper.

For information call 23954.

◆◆◆
TORRE DELL'OROLOGIO (CLOCK TOWER)
Piazza San Marco

The tower stands above the arch leading to the Mercerie shopping street close to the Basilica San Marco. Built at the end of the 15th century, its remarkable, brightly-enamelled clock-face and its digital clock are linked with automata, which attract crowds in the Piazza. On the summit of the tower two large bronze figures known as the *Mori* (Moors) strike the hour. During Ascension Week and at Epiphany, figures of the Magi emerge to either side of the clock-face and bow to the statue of the Madonna above it. Unfortunately, the Clock Tower has been closed to the public for the last five years for restoration purposes. It is unlikely that it will re-open in the foreseeable future. Check with the tourist office in Venice for the current position.

Scuole
The *scuole* of Venice were 'fraternity houses', where the more prosperous Venetians organised the city's welfare and administered charities. Many became elaborate treasure-houses of the arts and still contain some of the most remarkable collections of paintings in Venice, which reflects their prestige.

◆◆
SCUOLA GRANDE DEI CARMINI
near Campo Santa Margherita Dorsoduro beside the Carmelites' church

The Carmini had the elder Tiepolo as its principal decorator in the 18th century. Although the themes are, as usual, religious, his painting is sensual and so suited the mood of his time.

Open: 09.00 to 12.00 and 15.00 to 18.00 hours, Monday to Saturday.
Entrance charge.

◆◆◆
SCUOLA GRANDE DI SAN ROCCO ✓

Campo San Rocco, San Polo

This is the largest and grandest of the *scuole*, standing close to the church of the Frari. It is most celebrated for its great series of powerful paintings by Tintoretto depicting Biblical scenes. The whole interior is richly, indeed overpoweringly, decorated, carved and gilded.

Open: daily 09.00 to 17.00 hours.
Entrance charge.

SCUOLE/MUSEUMS AND GALLERIES

◆◆◆
SCUOLA DI SAN GIORGIO DEGLI SCHIAVONI

Calle Furlani, Castello
This has the early 16th-century artist Vittore Carpaccio's paintings as its main attraction. Downstairs in the little *scuola,* he painted an enchanting frieze illustrating the lives of three saints, St George, St Jerome and St Tryphon. There is also a painting of St Augustine in his study – an intimate glimpse into a medieval Venetian room.
Open: 10.00 to 12.30 and 15.30 to 18.00 hours, Tuesday to Sunday, 10.00 to 12.30 only on Monday.
Entrance charge.
Vaporetto: San Zaccaria.

Two magnificent *scuole* – **San Giovanni Evangelista,** Campiello di San Giovanni, San Polo, and **San Marco,** Campo San Giovanni e Paolo, Castello – are not generally open to the public but have splendid exteriors. The former, which is near the Frari, is approached through a beautiful marble arched screen; its interior is remarkable for a converging double staircase. Admission is possible when exhibitions are held, or sometimes on request. The latter, standing next to the church of San Zanipolo, now houses the main hospital and can be visited by appointment. However, its most interesting works of art, relief carvings incorporating startling perspectives, can be seen on the outside wall facing the *campo.*

Museums and Galleries

◆◆◆
ACCADEMIA
Campo della Carità, Dorsoduro
The most famous and comprehensive collection of Venetian painting is housed in this former church, monastery and *scuola* at the Dorsoduro side of the wooden Accademia Bridge (one of the three crossing points of the Canal Grande). Most of the paintings come from palaces and churches in the city and, although it would have been more appropriate to see them in their original settings, here they are grouped in galleries and are well lit.
Usually some galleries are closed for various reasons, but there is always enough on display to delight and even cause visual and mental indigestion. For those who like to visit a major gallery with a particular goal there is much to choose between. There is, for example, Giovanni Bellini's *Madonna Enthroned* and Carpaccio's *The Presentation of Jesus* in Room II, Giorgione's *Tempest* and Bellini's *Madonna of the Trees* in Room V; Titian's *St John the Baptist* in Room VI; three magnificent paintings by Veronese in Room XI; the Accademia's only Canaletto and six charming 18th-century *Scenes from Venetian Life* by Longhi in Room XVII; and Carpaccio's enchanting series of paintings illustrating *The Legend of St Ursula,* in which the clothes and settings are those of 15th-century Venice, in Room XXI.

A detail from the Carpaccio's epic St Ursula in the Accademia

Open: daily, 09.00 to 19.00 hours. However, the daily allocation of tickets are sold early in the day.
Entrance charge.
For information telephone 5222247.
Vaporetto: Accademia.

◆◆
CA' D'ORO GALLERIA FRANCHETTI (FRANCHETTI GALLERY)

Grand Canal, Cannaregio 3922
The most famous *palazzo* on the Grand Canal was named after the gilding of its elaborate façade when it was new. Its elaborate façade, still under long-term restoration but

MUSEUMS AND GALLERIES

Although no longer gilded, the Ca' d'Oro remains a magnificent example of Venetian architecture

without its original sumptuous furnishings, houses an elegant new gallery displaying Italian art, including frescos by Titian and Giorgione. Reopened in 1984, this magnificent building retains its architectural bones, but not its atmosphere.
Open: daily, 09.00 to 13.30 hours.
Entrance charge.

For information call 5238790.
Vaporetto: Ca' d'Oro.

◆
CA' PESARO GALLERIA D'ARTE MODERNA E MUSEO ORIENTALE (GALLERY OF MODERN ART AND ORIENTAL MUSEUM)
Canal Grande, Santa Croce
Worth visiting if only to see inside this enormous 17th-century baroque *palazzo* overlooking the Grand Canal. It was built for Giovanni Pesaro, who became Doge in 1658. It houses contemporary art

century palace overlooking the Grand Canal has been filled with furniture and paintings of the 18th century. The magnificent rooms of the *piano nobile* are richly decorated with gilding, frescos and painted ceilings, including one by Tiepolo. On the floor above can be seen paintings of Venetian life by Guardi and Longhi and a succession of small rooms, decorated with frescos by the younger Tiepolo. The top floor, which houses a collection of costumes, the stock of a pharmacist's shop and the marionette theatre, is often closed.

The poet Robert Browning occupied a suite of rooms below the *piano nobile* (not open to the public) and died there in 1889.

Open: 10.00 to 17.00 hours, Saturday to Thursday; closed Friday.
Entrance charge.
Vaporetto: Ca' Rezzonico.

◆
CASA GOLDONI (GOLDONI MUSEUM)

Calle dei Nomboli, San Polo 2793
The birthplace of the 18th-century Venetian playwright Carlo Goldoni was here in the Palazzo Centani. It has a charming courtyard with a Gothic stone staircase and handsome well-head, with Goldoni relics and the Institute of Theatrical Studies upstairs.
Open: daily, 08.30 to 13.30 hours.
Entrance free.
For further information telephone 5236353.
Vaporetto: San Toma.

exhibitions on the first two floors and oriental art on the top floor.
Open: 09.00 to 19.00 hours, Tuesday to Sunday.
Entrance charge.
Vaporetto: San Stae.

◆◆◆
CA ' REZZONICO MUSEO DEL SETTECENTO VENEZIANO (MUSEUM OF EIGHTEENTH-CENTURY VENICE) ✓

Grand Canal, Dorsoduro
This immensely grand 17th-

MUSEUMS AND GALLERIES

◆◆◆
COLLEZIONE (RACOLTA) GUGGENHEIM (GUGGENHEIM COLLECTION)

Calle Cristoforo, Dorsoduro 701

The collection of Cubist, Abstract and Surrealist art acquired by the late Peggy Guggenheim, the American millionairess, is housed in her former home, an unfinished 18th-century *palazzo* on the Canal Grande, Palazzo Venier de Leoni. Paintings and sculptures of the 20th century – including Peggy Guggenheim's own discovery, Jackson Pollock – will delight those who appreciate modern art, while those who do not will enjoy the view of the Grand Canal.

Open: 11.00 to 18.00 hours, Wednesday to Monday; closed on Tuesday.
Entrance charge.
For further information telephone 5206288.
Vaporetto: Accademia or Salute.

FORTUNY MUSEUM *see* MUSEO FORTUNY

FRANCHETTI GALLERY *see* CA ' D'ORO

GOLDONI MUSEUM *see* CASA GOLDONI

'The Angel of the City', one of the startling pieces in the Guggenheim Collection

GUGGENHEIM COLLECTION
see **COLLEZIONE GUGGENHEIM**

◆
MUSEO ARCHEOLOGICO (ARCHAEOLOGICAL MUSEUM)

Piazzo San Marco 17, San Marco
The museum contains a collection of original Greek and Roman sculpture, much of which was bought together in the 16th century. It is temporarily housed in the Procuratie Nuove, which adjoins the Marciana Library (closed to the public except the reading-room, which can be visited by telephoned application to 5208788).
Open: 09.00 to 14.00 hours, Monday to Saturday; 09.00 to 13.00 hours, Sunday and holidays.
Entrance charge.
For further information telephone 5225978.

◆◆
MUSEO CORRER (CORRER MUSEUM)

Piazza San Marco
The principal historical museum of the city runs above the arcade on the west and south sides of the Piazza and is entered by a wide marble staircase at the western end. The exhibits include paintings, models, costumes, books, arms and armour, much of it captured from the Turks. Particularly sinister is the lion's mask letter-box (*bocca di leone*) for written denunciations of enemies of the state. There are also relics of the *Bucintoro*, the huge, elaborate ceremonial galley used by the Doges.

Open: daily, 10.00 to 17.00 hours (last admission at 16.30 hours).
Entrance charge.
For further information telephone 5225625.
Vaporetto: San Marco.

◆◆
MUSEO FORTUNY (FORTUNY MUSEUM)

Campo San Benedetto, San Marco
The Palazzo Pesaro degli Orfei was the home and studio of the Spanish-born artist, sculptor, architect and dress-designer Mariano Fortuny (1871–1949). His studio contains a permanent exhibition of his work and is redolent of rich bohemian life in Venice at the turn of the century. Temporary exhibitions are also held in the 15th-century *palazzo,* which was bequeathed to the city by Fortuny's widow.
Open: daily except Monday, 09.00 to 19.00 hours.
Entrance charge.
For further information telephone 5200995
Vaporetto: San Angelo.

◆
MUSEO QUERINI-STAMPALIA

Campiello Querini, Castello
The Querini-Stampalia *palazzo* was the home of another grand Venetian family and 20 rooms are still furnished with their pictures and furniture. A list of exhibits may be borrowed. This and the Palazzo Mocenigo are two of many such palaces, illustrating the extraordinary richness of Venice at the height of its power.
Open: 10.00 to 12.30 and 15.30 to 18.00 hours, Tuesday to

MUSEUMS AND GALLERIES

This lion's mask door knocker guards the entrance to the Museo Storico Navale

Saturday; closed Monday.
Entrance charge.
For further information
telephone 5225235.
Vaporetto: San Zaccharia.

◆
MUSEO DI STORIA NATURALE (NATURAL HISTORY MUSEUM)
Fondaco dei Turchi, Canal Grande, Santa Croce
The museum is housed in the restored building once used by Turkish merchants. Many of the exhibits relate to the wildlife of the lagoon.
Open: 09.00 to 13.00 hours, Tuesday to Sunday; closed

Monday.
Entrance charge.
For further information
telephone 5240885.

◆◆
MUSEO STORICO NAVALE (NAVAL MUSEUM)
Campo San Biagio, Castello
The museum records the illustrious maritime past of Venice with a magnificent collection of ship models, pictures and relics housed in an old granary near the Arsenale, which was the naval base of the Republic (see page 46). The exhibits range from models of the galleys that fought the corsairs and Turks to the manned torpedoes used in World War II. There is a special section devoted to the gondola and other Venetian craft, with actual boats displayed in part of the Arsenale itself.
Open: daily, 09.00 to 13.00 hours.
Entrance charge.
For further information
telephone 5200276.
Vaporetto: Arsenale.

NAVAL MUSEUM *see* MUSEO STORICO NAVALE

◆◆
PALAZZO MOCENIGO (MOCENIGO PALACE)
Salizzada San Stae, Santa Croce 1992
This was the home of one of the grandest Venetian families until recent years and nine rooms of the 17th-century *palazzo*, decorated and furnished in the 18th century, remain much as it knew them. Richly gilded and painted,

these rooms, with their fine furniture and Murano glass chandeliers still have a private feeling about them. The building also houses a library and study collection of costume and fabrics and there is a small exhibition of antique Venetian textiles on view.

Open: 08.30 to 13.30 hours, Saturday.
Entrance charge.
Vaporetto: San Stae.

EXCURSIONS FROM VENICE (VENÉZIA)

Islands

Scattered across nearly 200 square miles (500 sq km) of the Venetian lagoon are some 40 islands. Half of them are now deserted, while those still

Lace-making in Burano is an ancient art still plied by the women of the island, who can be seen at work

inhabited may be thriving communities or isolated institutions – a prison, a hospital, or a religious retreat – and a few are used for public or private recreation. Enough of them can be visited to add another dimension to a holiday in Venice. There is public transport to the islands described, as well as organised tours to the main ones.

BURANO

The fishermen's and lace-makers' island with a population of about 5,000, lies more than five miles (8km) to the northeast of Venice. While Murano (see page 61) is workaday and slightly dishevelled, Burano is neat and clean and its multi-coloured cottages lining little canals make it a perfect

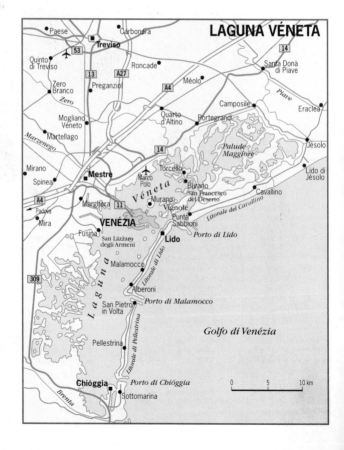

subject for photographs. Its character has been shaped by its industries – the robust way of life of its fishermen and boat-builders and the delicacy of its lace-makers' skills. Usually women can be seen making lace outside the doors of their cottages and their products (as well as embroidery from Hong Kong) are on sale at stalls and local shops.

There are few buildings of note but the church of **San Martino** contains a painting of *The Crucifixion* by the elder Tiepolo and boasts the most alarmingly tilted campanile of them all.

Vaporetto: route 12.

◆◆
CHIOGGIA

Once an island, Chioggia is now, like Venice, connected to the mainland by a causeway; unlike Venice, several of its canals have been filled in to become roads for cars. In the far south of the lagoon, 16 miles (25.5km) from Venice, it has grown from a fishing-port to an important town of some 55,000 inhabitants. Now, in essence, it belongs to the mainland rather than the lagoon.

Much of the town, particularly around the remaining canals, is reminiscent of Venice and many buildings date from the 13th to 18th centuries. There are several fine churches, notably the **Duomo**, built between the 13th and 17th centuries, which contains a painting by the elder Tiepolo. There are a number of

The colours of Burano could have come straight from the set of an Italian opera

excellent fish restaurants near the harbour and in the Corso del Popolo.

Vaporetto route 11 from the Lido (or by bus from the Piazzale Roma).

◆◆
THE LIDO

This is the only one of the Venetian islands to have roads, and its buses, cars and lorries are imported by ferry from the mainland. A little to the southeast of Venice, it is just over seven miles (11km) long and half a mile (1km) wide, covering the largest sand bank between the lagoon and the Adriatic. With a population of about 20,000 it is essentially a seaside holiday resort and is crowded in summer, when it also is host to the International Film Festival.

It was at its most fashionable before World War I as the architecture of its hotels and villas testifies, and its long sandy beach is still lined with wooden bathing-huts, which recall that time. Its most notable building is, in fact, a short distance across the water: the 16th-century **fortress of Sant' Andrea**, built on the little island of Vignole to command the main entrance to the lagoon. It was the guns of this fort that fired on a French warship in 1797, so precipitating the French invasion and the end of the Republic. The fortress, adorned with a massive relief carving of the Lion of St Mark, is currently under major restoration and not open to the public.

From the *vaporetto* bound from the Lido to San Marco, Venice is seen as it was intended it should first be seen, from the deck of a ship approaching from the sea, its towers, domes and palaces materialising between water and sky in one of the great spectacles the world has to offer.

Vaporetto: routes 1, 2, 6 and 34; 2 and 28 serving the Casino and 17 the westerly pier at San Nicolò near the entrance to the lagoon. From the *vaporetto* landing

The island of Murano is famous for its glass, but another attraction is S Donato and its elegant clocktower

stage of *Santa Maria Elizabetta*, ACTV buses leave for all destinations on the Lido. *Linea A* goes to the north; *Linea B*, to the public bathing beaches at San Nicolò; *Linea C*, to the northern end of the Lido; while *Linea 11* runs the entire length of the island.

◆◆
MURANO

With a population of nearly 8,000, Murano lies a short distance to the north of the city. It is an industrial island and has the feel of a small working town, although some of its factories lie derelict. Glass is its product and has been since the 13th century, when production was moved out of Venice itself because of the fire-risk. Venetian glass has long been a curious mixture of the beautiful and the vulgar, whether in table-glass, ornaments, mirrors or chandeliers.

Past products can be seen in the **Museo Vetrario di Murano**, Fondamenta Giustinian and Fondamenta Manin (tel: 739586).
Open: 10.00 to 17.00 hours, Thursday to Tuesday; closed Wednesday.
Entrance charge.

New production can be seen in many factory showrooms to which visitors will constantly be invited.

Murano is a miniature, shabbier Venice with its own scaled-down Canal Grande, crossed by a single bridge. Its most notable builiding is the church of **Santi Maria e Donato,** which has a 12th-century mosaic floor and a 15th-century 'ship's keel' roof. *Vaporetto* routes 5, 12 and 13.

◆
SAN FRANCESCO DEL DESERTO

This remote and peaceful island can be reached by ferry from Burano and the resident friars will show visitors the 13th-century cloister and the church of the hermitage, where St Francis of Assisi is said to have stayed.
Open: daily 09.00 to 11.00 hours and 15.00 to 17.00 hours. Donation on admission. Access is from Burano.

◆
SAN LAZZARO DEGLI ARMENI

This Armenian island can also be visited and the church, monastery and library seen. Lord Byron stayed there to learn Armenian.
Open: 15.00 to 17.00 hours, Sunday to Thursday. *Vaporetto* route 20.

◆
SAN MICHELE

This is the cemetery island, as can be seen by its sepulchral white walls and the tall, dark cypress trees beyond. The beautiful 15th-century church of **San Michele in Isola** is of interest to students of Renaissance artchitecture, but the cemetery (accessible from 07.30 to 16.00 hours) is even sadder than could be expected, for dead Venetians cannot rest there long. While the famous – such as the composer Stravinsky, the poet Ezra Pound and the ballet impresario Diaghilev – are allowed to remain, nearly all Venetians buried here are disinterred after a period and their bones scattered on a reef made of their ancestors' remains in a remote reach of the lagoon. The visitor cannot fail to be confronted by evidence that here death, as well as life, is transitory.
Vaporetto route 5.

◆◆◆ TORCELLO✓

Torcello was the first island to be settled by refugees from the barbarian invasion of the 5th century. At the height of its power, the population was said to have numbered 20,000 but the growth of the more distant and secure Venice, the silting of its creek and the prevalence of malaria reduced it to the level of the other small islands of the lagoon by the 15th century. Now its few score inhabitants grow vines and vegetables and run three notable restaurants. Lying close to the mainland marshes and more than six miles (9.5km) to the northeast of Venice, the little green island offers peace after the bustling city and relaxation in walks along its narrow footpaths. Its

'Judgement Day' – magnificent mosaics on the island of Torcello

great monument is the cathedral of **Santa Maria dell' Assunta**, where the extraordinary Byzantine mosaics – notably a tall and compelling *Madonna* and a vast depiction of *Judgement Day* – have just been restored.

The whole island, including the cathedral, the small church of **Santa Fosco**, the archaeological museum and the surrounding farmland, is easily explored and can be combined with lunch on a day-trip from Venice without making an early start or expecting a late return. *Vaporetto* route 12.

Mainland

Expeditions to the mainland can be made by train, bus, hired car and even by boat. The hinterland – the Veneto – was long ruled by Venice and so it is marked by Venetian taste both in its towns and in its country villas.

Italy's second oldest university town, Padova makes an ideal expedition to the mainland. Palazzo della Ragione stands between two colourful markets

♦♦♦

PADOVA (PADUA)

The nearest large town to Venice with a population of a quarter of a million, Padova can be reached by train, bus, car – or by boat. The latter, the *Burchiello* and its rival the *Ville del Brenta* sail between April and October from San Marco at about 09.00 (times and fares available from hotel concierges, travel agents and tourist information offices), cross the lagoon and cruise up

the Brenta Canal, which is, in fact, a river. Stopping at several magnificent Renaissance villas on its banks and for lunch at *Il Burchiello* restaurant, they arrive at Padua between 1800 and 1830, and the 23-mile (37km) return journey to Venice is made by bus or train.

A Venetian university city since the 15th century – and rich in buildings of that century – Padova is now dominated by commerce.

◆◆◆
VERONA

West of Vicenza (see below) and close to Lake Garda is Verona, famous as the setting of Shakespeare's play *Romeo and Juliet* and for its Roman remains, notably a magnificent arena, which is sometimes used for performances of opera.

◆◆◆
VICENZA

The capital of the Veneto is Vicenza, a good-looking city, for which the great architect Andrea di Palladio – a native of Padova – designed a dozen buildings. Now with a population of about 120,000, it lies 32 miles (51km) from Venice.

A smaller but equally busy town is **Treviso**, less than 20 miles (32km) from Venice and noted for its good and fashionable restaurants.

Hill-Towns

Northward from the lagoon stand the Alps with Austria beyond.

◆◆◆
ASOLO

The most beautiful of the hinterland towns, Asolo lies in the foothills of the Alps 40 miles (64km) from Venice. A charming town of some 6,000 inhabitants, its old houses – sometimes arcaded at street level as is the custom in hill-towns – cluster around squares and narrow streets and overlook a landscape decorated with villas and cypress trees.

Here also is one of the most celebrated hotels in Italy, the **Villa Cipriani** (tel: 0432 55444), where the food is what is expected from its name (see page 77).

For clean mountain air and stunning views, head north and explore the majestic Dolomites

◆◆◆
BASSANO DEL GRAPPA

In the foothills of the Alps, nearly 50 miles (80km) north-west of Venice, this town of 37,000 inhabitants was once under Venetian rule. Formerly renowned for its school of painting, it now produces colourful pottery, which is sold in Venice and throughout northern Italy.

There are some fine old buildings and a famous covered wooden bridge – the **Ponte Coperto** – which has been rebuilt several times since the early 13th century. Bassano is noted for the strong alcoholic spirit, *Grappa* and its

restaurants for game and mushrooms from the surrounding hills.

The town is a good centre for exploring the mountains – particularly **Monte Grappa**, which was an Italian stronghold during World War I – and the battlefields Ernest Hemingway described in *A Farewell to Arms.*

Further north and into the Alps is the handsome old town of **Belluno** and beyond it the mountain resort of **Cortina** – renowned for winter sports and summer walking – and the Dolomite mountains. Austria itself is just within range of a day's excursion.

◆
POSSAGNO

Anyone eager to see more works of art should visit the

village of Possagno, 45 miles (72km) northwest of Venice, the home of the sculptor Antonio Canova. Born here in 1757, Canova became the greatest of the neoclassical sculptors, producing smoothly graceful figures and delicate portraits, which are now in galleries throughout the world.

His house is now the centre of a gallery devoted to his works, mostly plaster models for statuary, and in the parish church which he gave to the village – the **Tempio di Canova**, inspired by the Parthenon in Athens and the Pantheon in Rome – is his tomb. But only his body lies there; his heart remains in Venice, within the pyramid he himself designed for Titian in the great church of the Frari (see page 33).

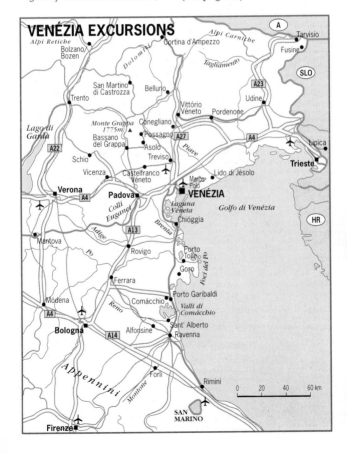

EXCURSIONS:GOING EAST

Going East

LIDO DI JÉSOLO

Along the Adriatic coast to the east of Venice is the seaside resort, which has a good beach and caters principally for package holidays. It is reached by bus from Venice.

The Roman Theatre at Trieste, evidence of its ancient beginnings

TRIESTE

Further east of Venice than Lido di Jésolo is the great seaport of Trieste, once part of the Austro-Hungarian Empire and now connected with Venice by rail.

A little further to the north, just across the Slovenian border, is **Lipica**, where the Lipizzaner white horses are bred and can be ridden.

PEACE AND QUIET

Countryside and Wildlife in and around Venice

by Paul Sterry

For an island city so completely dominated by buildings, Venice might seem an unpromising destination for the holiday naturalist. Venice and the Veneto coast have considerable wildlife interest and the city makes a good base from which to explore the watery habitat surrounding it. Venice lies in the Laguna Veneta, a marine lagoon near the mouth of the River Po which is almost completely cut off from the sea by sand bars. The lagoon is studded with islands and saltmarsh, the whole area being a haven for wildlife, in particular birds. Ducks, waders, egrets and herons are all numerous at certain times of the year. Although much of the Po delta and Laguna Veneta are inaccessible, many species can be seen during boat trips or from the adjacent mainland. By way of a complete contrast, those who want a few days' break from Venice can make a comparatively short journey north through sunny hillsides to the Italian Alps.

Venice and the Venetian Lagoon

Visitors to Venice might be forgiven for supposing that, after people, pigeons and cats are not just the commonest residents of the city but its *only* living inhabitants. However true this might seem at first glance, a more thorough tour of even the city itself will turn up a surprising number of birds, and a boat tour to one of the other islands is sure to enthral.

Parks and gardens, however small, in the quieter backstreets of Venice are likely to host serins. These delightful little relatives of the canary sing a beautiful, twittering song throughout spring and early summer, usually from the topmost branches of a tree. Search the lower branches and dense foliage of bushes and you may find a variety of warblers; melodious warblers, blackcaps, lesser whitethroats and even Sardinian warblers can all be seen. Although the spring migration period is the best time of year for seeing these birds, some of them linger on into the summer months.

Black redstarts are also found in parks and gardens but are equally at home on the roofs of houses. Some individuals can become quite confiding and seem not to be bothered at all by people. Gulls frequent the shores of the lagoon and sometimes congregate where boats and larger ships are moored. The yellow-legged race of herring gull is most often seen in the winter months but black-headed gulls are frequent all year round. Scrutinise each one carefully because the somewhat similar Mediterranean gull is also often numerous. In its summer plumage, this is one of the most elegant of gulls and sports a black hood, red eye-

PEACE AND QUIET

Black redstarts are equally at home in the countryside or the city

ring and pure white wings. It has a distinctive 'cow-cow' call. Boat trips between the islands in the Laguna Veneta pass the occasional undisturbed shoreline and areas of reedbed. Waders, grey herons and little egrets, the latter species easily recognised by its white plumage, black legs and bright yellow feet, prefer the open shores. Marsh harriers and purple herons, on the other hand, favour the sanctuary provided by the reeds.

Unfortunately, boat trips generally offer only fleeting glimpses of these habitats and to study them in more detail it is probably best to return to mainland Italy and explore the Po delta from there.

The Po Delta, Valli di Comacchio and Punte Alberte

To the south of Venice and the Laguna Veneta lies the delta of the River Po, which drains into the Gulf of Venice. At one time, the wetland areas along the coast would have been continuous and would have comprised vast areas of brackish lagoons and saltmarsh. However, centuries of exploitation have affected many of the more accessible areas of the River Po's valley and delta and reduced its value to wildlife: commercial development and changed land use of landward regions have encouraged the growth of towns and vast acreages of rice fields and other agricultural land.

Despite man's influence on the valley of the River Po, considerable areas of the delta's coastal fringe still remain largely untouched. Some are protected by their inaccessibility, others by reserve status as with the Riserva Naturale Bocche di Po, north of Ravenna. These wetlands are a haven for breeding, migrant and wintering birds and, despite the inevitable difficulties in viewing such a water-bound region, boat tours from Porto Tolle or Goro and coastal roads afford tantalising but exciting glimpses of the wildlife. Spring in the Po delta sees the arrival of thousands of migrant birds from their wintering grounds in Africa. Black terns, with smaller numbers of whiskered terns and white-winged black terns are sometimes seen in small flocks catching insects over open water. Their larger relatives, Caspian terns and common terns, dive for fish and crustaceans and are occasionally seen with the smallest member of the gull family in Europe, the little gull. Shallow water around lagoon margins and at the edges of islands, attracts a wide variety of wading birds which feed mainly on small invertebrates and fish. Most elegant of these is the black-winged stilt, whose long, red legs allow it to feed in deeper water than its equally distinctive relative, the avocet. This latter species has black and white plumage and a thin, upturned bill which is scythed through the water. Ruff, redshanks, marsh sandpipers, dunlin and Temminck's stints also pass through in spring and

many stop off on autumn migration as well to feed and rest. Although each species has its own preferred habitat, mixed flocks are often seen, testing the identification skills of most birdwatchers.

The Valli di Comacchio is a large brackish lagoon situated between the mouth of the River Po and Ravenna to the south. Almost all the species found in the Po delta also occur here, but access to this enormous area is effectively restricted to viewing from the road between Porto Garibaldi on the coast and Comacchio, or the road which runs along the west side of the lagoon from Comacchio south to Alfonsine.

The stately great egret is an

The elegant grey heron can be spotted off the more remote islands

occasional winter visitor to the Valli di Comacchio but more frequent in the summer months is its smaller relative, the little egret. Undisturbed breeding habitat for this bird, and many other species of heron, has been drastically reduced over the years but at the Oasi di Protezione di Punte Alberte (Wildlife Oasis of Punte Alberte), healthy populations of egrets, herons and ducks can be found. Situated between the Valli di Comacchio and Ravenna, and managed by the Italian branch of the World Wide Fund for Nature, Punte Alberte can be viewed by the public from its perimeter. For access to the reserve itself and its

Watch out for the bright green tree frog among the vegetation

observation tower, contact the WWF for further information.

The Po Valley

The low-lying land that forms the valley of the River Po dominates the whole of northern Italy and stretches from Turin in the west to the Venetian coast in the east. This huge area with its fertile soils is, understandably, subject to intensive cultivation, but this is not always to the detriment of wildlife. Flooded fields support large numbers of water birds while marshes, wet meadows, lakes and even drainage ditches harbour colourful plants, fish and amphibians if you look carefully.

The rice fields, which are such a feature of much of the Po valley, offer rich feeding for birds. Grey herons, purple herons, night herons and little egrets as well as black-winged stilts and other migrant waders can be found in most areas. However, their abundance and exact distribution is dependent upon the time of year and the precise environmental conditions: seasonal planting or harvesting may cause the birds to move to new areas. In winter, wildfowl, lapwings and snipe arrive in large numbers from northern Europe and boost the numbers of resident species.

Drainage ditches and stream margins soon become overgrown with reeds and other emergent vegetation and are a sanctuary for wildlife. The colourful caterpillars of swallowtail butterflies feed on the leaves of umbellifers. Tree

Little bitterns are more difficult to find, living among the reeds at the water's edge

frogs clamber through the vegetation while agile frogs remain in the safety of the waters below. Marsh warblers, crakes and little bitterns are secretive residents, while great reed warblers often announce their presence by singing from a prominent perch. Patches of woodland are the haunt of golden orioles and nightingales and also attract passage migrant species in spring and autumn. Penduline tits also like woodland borders and build their curious, flask-shaped nests suspended from the end of an overhanging branch. Agriculture has fortunately left some areas comparatively untouched. Water meadows, although an increasingly rare sight, are home to colourful butterflies and may host flowers such as marsh orchids, Jersey orchids, gladioli and many more.

Open Country

The journey north from Venice leads eventually to the foothills of the Italian Alps, but before this mountainous region is reached, the visitor will find attractive, rolling countryside. Still feeling the influence of the Mediterranean climate, the land enjoys hot summers and mild winters and is

PEACE AND QUIET

The distinctive markings of the swallowtail larva on milk parsley

consequently dotted with olive groves and vineyards. In spring, colourful flowers and butterflies abound and birds find a haven here as well. Tilled soils untouched by herbicides become a riot of colour in spring: poppies, corn marigolds, asphodels, bugloss, grape hyacinths, star thistles and gladioli can all be abundant under the right conditions. Although the heat of summer withers the vegetation to a uniform brown, the few weeks in spring when plants are in flower more than make up for the months of desiccation. Of course, wildflowers are colourful and fragrant not for our benefit, but to attract insects which serve as pollinating agents. Chafer beetles, hummingbird hawk moths and butterflies such as swallowtails, scarce swallowtails, dappled white,

black-veined white and green hairstreak are frequent visitors, some falling victim to praying mantises or crab spiders.

The bare soils of vineyards are favoured feeding grounds for birds such as crested lark, short-toed lark, tawny pipit and that most typically Mediterranean bird, the hoopoe. These can be difficult to spot since they feed unobtrusively on the ground, but easier to find are woodchat shrikes, lesser grey shrikes and red-backed shrikes. Although these attractively marked species are songbirds, they behave like miniature birds of prey, perching on wires and posts and swooping down on unsuspecting prey such as beetles and grasshoppers. They also have the rather macabre habit of impaling their larger catches so that they can be more easily torn up.

Black-eared wheatears and

corn buntings are also found in this rolling countryside. The jingling song of the latter species is a familiar sound as is the twittering song of the serin. Unmistakeable and truly evocative of the Mediterannean, however, is the bubbling call of the bee-eater. As its name suggests, the bee-eater does indeed catch insects, and parties of these extraodinarily colourful birds are often seen gliding and swooping over vineyards, orchards and olive groves.

The Italian Alps

Popular both with residents of the Venetian coast and visitors to Veneto, the Italian Alps are a frequent weekend destination during the winter skiing season. In addition to the attraction of winter sports, the Alps offer spectacular scenery and wildlife to match this grandeur. Although winter is the 'high' season, a visit during the summer can be equally worth while, plants and animals abound and temperatures are warm and pleasant. This can make a refreshing change from Venice where the heat during July and August can be oppressive.

Despite increasing public pressure, the Alps remain Italy's last wilderness region. Cloaked in forests of beech, hazel and Scots pine at lower elevations, arolla pines, white firs and larches grow to the tree line at about 6,000 feet (1,800m). Above this, scree slopes and colourful alpine meadows cover the landscape,

restricted only by the line of permanent snow fields and glaciers which blanket the highest peaks.

Although almost any area of the Alps is worth exploring, a few areas in particular deserve a special mention. The **Foresta Tarvisio** (Tarvisio Forest) and adjacent **Parco Naturale di Fusine** (Fusine Natural Park), close to the Slovenian and Austrian borders in the Julian Alps have forests, high mountains and beautiful lakes. The **Riservas Naturale Val Tovanella, Schiara Occid** and **Monti del Sole** and the **Parco Naturale Panveggio-Pale di San Martino** near Belluno are also stunningly attractive and are especially good for flowers while the **Parco Naturale Adamello-Brenta** near Trento may still support a small population of European brown bears, now sadly on the verge of extinction.

From May until July, alpine meadows are colourful with flowers such as spring gentian, trumpet gentian, alpine snowbell, edelweiss, bird's-eye primrose and globeflower, and are the haunt of alpine marmots, alpine choughs, snow finches and chamois. Water pipits, rock thrushes, ptarmigan and alpine accentors favour the scree and boulder slopes while golden eagles and the occasional griffon vulture circle overhead on the lookout for carrion. At least part of the eagle's diet is also live prey, which may include high altitude species, such as alpine hares and young chamois.

PEACE AND QUIET

The wooded lower slopes provide sanctuary for red deer, roe deer, red squirrels and a wide variety of forest birds. Citril finches usually nest near the tree line while lower down, Bonelli's warblers, crested tits, treecreepers, nutcrackers and hazelhens can be found, the latter, however, only by luck and persistent searching. Several species of woodpecker also occur in the Italian Alps, including white-backed and three-toed woodpeckers, as well as the

Birds-eye primrose; just one of the bright flowers of summer

largest European species, the black woodpecker. Spring is the best season for seeing woodpeckers as well as most other woodland birds, because at this time of year they are displaying or singing at the start of the breeding season. Glades and forest rides are good places to look for woodland flowers in spring and summer. Bellflowers, spiked rampion, purple coltsfoot and several species of orchids occur, including the attractive but distinctly local lady's slipper orchid. It goes without saying that none of these species should be picked.

FOOD AND DRINK

Its reputation for dull, unimaginative cooking, high prices and surly service is not fair to Venice. It is true that restaurants tend to be more expensive than those on the mainland, since almost everything but some of the fish has to be imported by barge; and along the tourist trails the waiters can become as jaded as their customers, particularly in summer.

That said, the visitor can eat well in Venice. Those enjoying the higher *trattoria* style of cooking will not be disappointed. Venetian restaurants offer the same range of basic Italian dishes as will be found throughout the country but their local specialities are more simple than those of, say, Florence, Bologna or Rome. For a first course try fish soup – *zuppa di pesce* – which is so full of shellfish, shrimps and white fish that it is best followed by something light; or Parma ham – *prosciutto crudo* – with fresh figs.

Two of the most familiar Venetian main dishes are acquired tastes: sliced calves' liver with onion (*fegato alla Veneziana*) and squid (*seppie*) cooked in its own black ink with cornmeal cake (*polenta*). Venetians are good at creating delectable sweets, particularly the light and creamy *tiramisú*, a delicious cold confection of chocolate, coffee, marscapone cheese and brandy.

Another way to get a taste of Italian food is to try some of the many local snacks (*cichetti*) available, usually displayed on counters. These include garlicky meatballs (*polpette*), mini-pizzas (*pizzetas*), various types of seafood and slices of fried vegetables.

When ordering drinks, '*una ombra*' (which means 'shade') will produce a glass of white house wine, unless you request *rosso* (red). *Ombra* comes from the old tradition of drinking wine in the shade of the Piazza. For a detailed description of Venetian food, read *Taste of Venice* by Jeanette Nance Nordio (published by Michael Joseph).

Restaurants

Restaurants in the middle and upper-middle range are generally cheaper than their equivalents in Britain and waiters are more often friendly than not. Many restaurants display a set-price *menu turistico* offering a choice of three or four dishes (*piatti*) for each course; this can be an inexpensive way of tasting a number of Venetian specialities. There are some 300 restaurants in the city. Some close in the low seasons and many shut on Sundays and Mondays, except those in hotels and the grander of these serve food suitable to their style, often out of doors in summer. Particularly recommended are the restaurants in the **Gritti Palace**, the **Danieli**, the **Monaco e Grand Canal** and the **Londra Palace** (see **Hotels**, pages 90–2).

The Cipriani Restaurants

Venetian restaurants owe much

FOOD AND DRINK

to the Cipriani family, who have given them a smart yet friendly style. The hotel named after them is now owned by Sea Containers, which also runs the Orient Express, but the family still run three notable restaurants which deserve pride of place, although they do now tend to be more expensive and attract the 'in-crowd'.

Harry's Bar, Calle Vallaresso, San Marco 1323 (tel: 5236797). This was the original Cipriani establishment, a favourite haunt of Ernest Hemingway, who would eat and drink in the downstairs bar, which is more amusing than the grander restaurant upstairs. It still has an air of the 1930s as do many of its customers – the richer expatriate residents of the city and the more eccentric and affluent Venetians – and there is often so much to watch indoors that nobody tries to look out of the opaque windows at the view. The food is delicious and quite expensive, although it is difficult to improve on a very simple meal of their speciality, *tagliolini verdi gratinati* (green pasta with chopped ham in a cheese sauce) and a jug of chilled Soave white wine from the Veneto.

Harry's Dolci, Fondamento San Biagio, Giudecca 773 (tel: 5224844).

Over on Giudecca island, the same management have opened a restaurant – originally designed as a tea-room – next to their own bakery. This serves much the same sort of food as Harry's Bar, but with emphasis on

sweets and cakes, as the word *dolci* implies. In summer, tables are set beside the water to command the view of passing ships and the Zattere waterfront beyond.

Locanda Cipriani (tel: 730150) The third and most delectable endowment by this family is on the island of Torcello to the northeast of Venice itself. It is open from Wednesday to Sunday between mid-March and October. Another favourite of Hemingway's, this looks like a country inn from the outside but is a smart restaurant within. Its particular joy is lunch outside among the flowers and vegetables of the walled garden with the tower of the cathedral just beyond. Again the food is Cipriani-style and fairly expensive but in fine, warm weather a meal here – combined with a visit to the cathedral and the voyage from Venice and back – can be a high-point of a holiday.

Eating by the Water

Waterside meals are a particular Venetian pleasure and these can be enjoyed on the Zattere or by quiet canals. There is a row of relatively cheap and cheerful *pizzerie* lining the *fondamenta* at this end of the Zattere, with tables on wooden platforms built out over the water. Here, beside the bridge over the San Trovaso canal, pizza with wine followed by ice-cream and coffee provides an excuse for sitting an hour or so in the sun, and is not expensive. No reservations. **Caffé Orientale**, Calle dell'

Spend a lazy lunch by the waterside

Olio, San Polo 2426 (tel: 719804). Eating on a little terrace beside a quiet canal in the centre of the city is a pleasure offered here. Once a charmingly old-fashioned *trattoria*, it has been renamed after a famous Venetian café and converted into a smart restaurant specialising in fish. The food is good and quite expensive and the décor coldly chic, the waterside tables adding the necessary Venetian character.

Riviera, Zattere, Dorsoduro

FOOD AND DRINK

1473 (tel: 5227621). This restaurant has been opened in a former religious building (on the façade stands a statue of a saint with a pig beside him; he is the patron saint of sausage-makers). In fine weather, tables are set outside by the water and the delicious food is slightly cheaper than at Cipriani restaurants.

Garden Restaurants
Gardens being much more unusual than water in Venice, restaurants with the former rightly make much of eating beneath a vine in a sun-dappled courtyard, or under Venetian lanterns at night.
Al Giardinetto, Calle della Regina, Santa Croce 2253 (tel: 721301). Small, simple and very resonably priced, it serves meals in its courtyard. Handy for the Hotel San Cassiano (see **Hotels**, page 93).
Da Ignazio, Calle dei Saoneria, San Polo 749 (tel: 5234852). On the same side of the Canal Grande as the Trattoria Nono Risorto (see below), this is another courtyard restaurant.
Montin, Fondamenta di Borgo, Dorsoduro 1147 (tel: 5227151). Among the best-known garden restaurants, it has a large garden and is cheerful and cosy inside when too cold for eating outdoors. It is difficult to find in a quiet and charming district near the Campo San Barnaba, but so popular that booking is usually essential.
Trattoria Nono Risorto, Campo San Cassiano, Santa Croce 2331 (tel: 5241169). Close to the Rialto markets, this

is another restaurant with a large garden, which also displays the work of contemporary artists. Like Montin, this specialises in simple Venetian dishes such as spaghetti with shellfish, mixed fried fish, squid with *polenta* and liver *Veneziana*.

Others
As an alternative to looking at water or boats, the passing throng is also a Venetian pleasure and some restaurants have tables out in a *campo.* Amongst many cheerful, unpretentious and typically Venetian *trattorie* is **Al Bacareto**, San Marco 3447 (tel: 5289336), close to Campo Santo Stefano.
Ai Corazzieri, Salizzada dei Corazzieri, Castello 3839 (tel: 5289859). This small but charming restaurant is hidden away behind the Campo Bandiera e Moro and the La Residenza hotel (see **Hotels**, page 93). Here one of the most delicious Venetian dishes is *tagliolini con cappe sante*: pasta with 'saints' heads', small scallops in piquant sauce.
Ai Gondolieri, Dorsoduro 366 (tel: 5286396). This is a new restaurant seriously specialising in Venetian cooking and situated between the Accademia bridge and the Collezione Guggenheim (see **Museums**, page 54).

Each district has its own little restaurants and there will always be several near each bed-and-breakfast hotel. Tourist menus with dishes at less than the à la carte prices are usually satisfactory but are unlikely to include the more interesting specialities. In restaurants of any class it is permissible to order pasta as a main course, so reducing the cost of the meal.

It can be assumed that the bill will include a service charge but Venetians do generally add an extra 1,000 *lire* a head as a further tip for the waiter.

Cafés, Bars and Snack Bars

Cafés have long played an important part in Venetian life, particularly in the exchange of news and gossip. In the Piazza San Marco, **Florian**, Castello 5719 (tel: 5285338), which

Valpolicella, one of the best red wines from the Veneto, is a perfect accompaniment to local dishes such as those seen here

FOOD AND DRINK

A drink in Piazza S Marco is expensive – so, like the atmosphere, make it an experience to savour

opened in 1720, was a centre of political dissent during Austrian rule in the 19th century, while the Austrians themselves patronised **Quadri**, Piazza San Marco 120-4 (tel: 5222105) on the opposite side of the square and their orchestras still compete for attention. Both are expensive and the cost of a cup of coffee at either should be regarded as the price of an experience of street theatre. In cold weather, the interior of Florian – all faded plush and 19th-century murals – is redolent of the last century.

At any café, bar or snack bar, a seat at a table usually doubles the bill but many of the smaller establishments serve only at the bar and lack even chairs.

SHOPPING

Venice has always been a city
for shopping. Over the
centuries its merchants made
the city's fortune by selling
wholesale the merchandise of
the East to fellow-Europeans;
now its hundreds of enticing
little shops sell Venetian arts
and crafts and the produce of
Italy to visitors.

There are no department
stores in Venice so shopping
can be combined with
sightseeing throughout the city.
The most fashionable shopping
areas are in and to the north
and west of the Piazza San
Marco and on and around the
Rialto bridge; the busiest,
along the wide Strada Nuovo
leading from the railway station
into the heart of the city. All
over Venice attractive little
shops can be found,
sometimes combined with
workshops making the goods
on sale. While the windows of
clothes shops and shoe shops
will catch the eye with their
displays of the latest fashions
from Rome and Milan, visitors
may want to take home
something that is peculiarly
Venetian. Some ideas may be
found in the sections below.
Most shops accept the major
credit cards and will pack and
mail or freight purchases to
their final destination.

Fabrics

As can be seen in the paintings
of Venetian life in past
centuries, richly coloured and
textured fabrics were always
favoured. They still are and a
new process of printing part-
rayon fabric with traditional

All the major hotels have bars,
of course, but the most
celebrated in the city is **Harry's
Bar**, Calle Vallaresso, San
Marco 1323 (tel: 5236797), near
the San Marco *vaporetto* pier
(see page 77). The speciality is
the Bellini – peach juice and
champagne – and the house
wines are excellent. It also
serves the most succulent (and
expensive) sandwiches; indeed
these are usually good, and with
generous fillings, in many
Venetian bars.

Venetian designs has produced a new range suitable for curtains, loose covers, cushion-covers and bedspreads. An attractive showroom for this is at the edge of the Grand Canal near the Ca'Rezzonico *vaporetto* pier: **Arianna da Venezia**, Dorsoduro 2793 (tel: 5221535). Another is near the Campo San Stefano: **Gaggio**, Calle delle Botteghe, San Marco 3451 (tel: 5228574). Some of the patterns are those favoured by the designer and artist Mariano Fortuny (1871–1949), best remembered for the light, pleated silk dresses he produced. His fabric designs are the speciality of **V Trois**, Campo San Maurizio, San Marco 2666 (tel: 5222905). Lace is made and sold by the women of the island of Burano beyond Murano.

Glass

Surprisingly, the Venetians, who have always had such good taste in art and architecture, have turned out a remarkable amount of vulgar nick-nacks during their millennium of glass-making. Today the bulk of the glass on display in shop windows and showrooms is over-ornate, ostentatious and impractical; vast ornaments, dinky souvenirs and wineglasses that are difficult to use and easy to break. That said, it is worth searching for the beautiful pieces that are still made with a purity of design and strong Venetian character.
For eight centuries, Murano

has been the glass-making island. Glass shops and showrooms abound in the city itself but when a visitor is invited to watch glass-blowing there, it will only be a demonstration in a back room: for the real thing, Murano must be visited and there, too, are the most comprehensive showrooms. Take time in choosing glass and do not be deflected by sales-talk which has been polished over the centuries. After a purchase, retailers and manufacturers are efficient at packing and freighting it.
For most people, the more strongly made and well-designed jugs, wineglasses and vases are the best buys. Children love the little glass animals, figures and trinkets that are often made in the glass shops themselves.
On Murano – reached by *vaporetto* from the Fondamenta Nuove, or by a *circolare* ferry from elsewhere in the city (see **Getting About**, pages 111–13) – the leading manufacturers are **Barovier e Toso**, Fondamenta Vetrai 28, Murano (tel: 739049), and elegant table glass can be bought from **Toso Vetri d'Arte**, Fondamenta Manin 1, Murano (tel: 736843) and **Nason e Moretti**, Fondamenta Serenella 12, Murano (tel: 939020). The most comprehensive showroom on the island is **CAM** in the Piazzale Colonna (tel: 739944). In the city itself the best-known glass shops are in and around the Piazza San Marco and a particularly wide selection is displayed by **Battison**, Calle

*The master of glass ornaments,
Amadi; at work on a delicate glass
bird*

Vallaresso, San Marco 1320
(tel: 5230509), near the San
Marco *vaporetto* pier. An
expedition to the far side of the
Canal Grande will find the
finest maker of glass
ornaments – exquisite birds,
insects and fruit – made in the
little shop, **Amadi**, Calle
Saoneri, San Polo 2747 (tel:
38089).
Glass costume jewellery is
often cheap and attractive and
antique Venetian glass beads
are sometimes made up as

ear-rings and brooches, as at
the **Beads Shop**, Calle San
Provolo, Castello 4719A (tel:
5286946).

Leather
Fine leatherwork is, of course,
an Italian speciality and there
are many smart shops selling
handbags, briefcases, belts and
shoes throughout the city. One
particularly elegant shop is
Vogini, Calle Ascensione, San
Marco 1257A – 1301 (tel:
5222573), close to the San
Marco *vaporetto* pier. For
supremely elegant and
expensive shoes, at least look at
the window displays of **Renè**,

Merceria San Salvador, San Marco 4983 (tel: 5229766). To see a typical shop and workshop combined, visit **Cose di Pelle**, Campo Santa Margherita, Dorsoduro 2946.

Metalwork

Small foundries and smithies still abound in the alleys of Venice, notably to the north of the Campo San Barnaba. They not only manufacture brass souvenirs – such as Lion of St Mark paperweights – but make practical and attractive coat-hooks, door-knockers and so on. Some of the old-established workshops also stock antique metalwork, which is not expensive. One such is **Rossetin Sergio**, Ca'Foscari, Dorsoduro 3230 (tel: 5224195). There are many silver shops and some silversmiths throughout the city. Most of their stock is manufactured elsewhere – such as the charming little silver boxes fashioned like sea shells – but a

Masks for the carnival or to give as presents – Tragicomica has hundreds

few both manufacture and sell, amongst them **Sfriso**, Campo San Toma, San Polo 2849 (tel: 5223558).

Paper

The fashion for marbled Italian paper applied to book covers, picture frames, stationery holders, blotters, pencils, ornaments and so on has taken hold of Venice and such shops often sell beautifully-coloured silk scarves and ties as well. A particularly elegant stock of hand-printed paper and silk is offered by **Alberto Valese-Ebru** at three shops, Salizzada San Samuele, San Marco 3135 (tel: 5200921), Calle della Fenice, San Marco 1920 (tel: 5286302) and San Stefano 3471. Another with a particularly wide range of paper is **Legatoria Piazzesi**, Santa Maria del Giglio, San Marco 2511C (tel: 5221205).

During the decade since the revival of the winter carnival, mask-shops and mask-makers have proliferated. Many of those produced are over-elaborate and have lost the charm and sophistication of masks made when the fashion was first revived. However, unpainted, white *papier-mâché* masks, which can be painted by the purchaser, are offered by **Ca'Macana**, Dorsoduro 3172, close to the Ca'Rezzonico (tel: 5203229) and masks can be seen being decorated at **La Mano,** Calle Longa, Castello 5175 (tel: 29995)

Masks and costumes for the carnival can be bought from **Tragicomica**, Campiello dei Meloni, San Polo 1414 (tel: 721102) and at **Balo Coloc**, Calle del Scaleter, San Polo 2235, which also stocks a remarkable range of hats.

Woodwork

Venetian craftsmen have produced painted and gilded furniture and frames for centuries, usually to charming baroque designs, and they still do. Furniture can be expensive and generally has to be freighted to its destination but frames for pictures and mirrors are often cheap, charming and more portable. Shops and workshops are scattered throughout the city but there are a number in the alleys to the immediate north and east of the Campo San Barnaba, one such being **Manuela Canestrelli**, San Barnaba, Dorsoduro 2779 (tel: 5230602). Another in the Campo San Stefano on the far side of the Accademia bridge is **Gianni Cavalier**, San Marco 2863A (tel: 5238621).

Other shoppers are also catered for.

Books

Books about Venice in English are an important part of the stock at **Libreria Internazionale Sangiorgio**, Calle Larga XXII Marzo, San Marco 2087 (tel: 5238451). Another well-stocked shop is **Libreria Sansovino**, Piazza di San Marco 84 (tel: 5222623). A pleasant shop, 'which stocks English, French and German books is **Il Librario a San Barnaba**, Fondamenta Gheradini, Dorsoduro 2835A (tel: 5228737).

SHOPPING

Fashion

There are so many smart clothes shops in Venice that the fashion-conscious can spend a day window-shopping instead of looking at Old Master paintings. The well-known **Emporio Armani**, Calle dei Fabri, San Marco 989A, is a good place to start the exploration. In the unlikely event of disappointment, visitors have been known to find exactly what they want in a smart boutique in the departure lounge at Marco Polo Airport on their way home: this **Boutique di Vittorio Testi** is particularly good for men's ties.

Fresh fish from the lagoon is a speciality of some restaurants

Food and Wine

The principal food markets are at the western (San Polo) end of the Rialto Bridge, where fruit and vegetables are sold every morning except Sunday and fish daily except Sunday and Monday. Most of the fish is imported frozen but some – often live – is direct from the lagoon and the Adriatic. Near by are several small shops selling a variety of cheese. Other fruit, vegetable and fish stalls are often to be found in the Strada Nuova (leading into the city from the railway station), in several *campi* – including Campo Santa Margherita – and there is a barge selling fruit and vegetables moored in the canal alongside the Campo San Barnaba. Grocers' shops, butchers and bakers are scattered throughout the city. The wines of the Veneto – and those from farther afield – are sold in grocers' shops throughout the city.

Markets

Stalls selling silk scarves and ties and leather goods are set up at either end of the Rialto Bridge, upon which are two parallel rows of little shops selling jewellery, leather goods, silks and shoes. Stalls are also found in the Strada Nuova and those selling souvenirs congregate along the Riva degli Schiavoni; these include artists mass-producing views of Venice and offering instant caricatures. About twice a year an antiques market is held in the Campo San Maurizio.

ACCOMMODATION

There are about 200 hotels in Venice and, this being Italy, most of them are well run. A few may have become slatternly through over-confidence induced by a non-stop flow of package tourists, but their principal handicap is age. A medieval palace, religious institution or merchant's house cannot be converted into a modern hotel with identical bedrooms, although ruthless use of steel joists has opened up many a spacious lobby behind a Renaissance façade. Thus the same hotel is likely to offer both large and lofty bedrooms commanding magnificent views and dark poky rooms overlooking a dank ventilation well or an alley. If a particular hotel is known to command fine views, suitable rooms can usually be reserved at an extra charge. Lone travellers are particularly at risk since single rooms are the most cramped. One solution for those accustomed to travelling alone and staying in the more expensive hotels is to choose one that is less expensive and book a double room.

Venice is a remarkably quiet city but for light sleepers there is the hazard of church bells in the early morning and the hooters and bellowing diesels of barges on the wider canals. For most visitors the chance of such disturbance is an acceptable risk.

Now that the city is busy at Christmas and Easter and the February carnival has been

Near the Palazzo Ducale, the Danieli is Venice's largest hotel, boasting such visitors as Dickens and Wagner

reintroduced, there are fewer times of year when it can seem empty. These currently are November, the first three weeks of December, January and March, when some hotels may close. The busiest months are July, August and September.

Most Venetian hotels now serve only breakfast and only the grandest offer a cooked breakfast. A number have good restaurants but, as a general rule, half-board should be avoided because this nearly always involves the evening meal and so hampers the enjoyable exploration of the

ACCOMMODATION

city's restaurants (see pages 77–83).

The tourist information offices at Piazzale Roma (in the Autorimessa Communale garage); on the Tronchetto; at Santa Lucia railway station; Marco Polo airport; and the Venice exit of the autostrada at Marghera all operate a hotel booking service (see **Directory** section for exact location and office hours). If a room is found the 10,000 *lire* deposit is deducted from your first night's bill.

Expensive Hotels

There are a dozen very grand hotels in Venice, most of them, suitably, on the Grand Canal near San Marco.

Bauer Grünwald e Grand Hotel, Campo San Moisè, San Marco 1459 (tel: 5207022). The land-side of this hotel is modern but its canal façade reveals that it was once a splendid palazzo. Today it has an opulence designed for the plutocracy. It offers views over the Grand Canal.

Bonvecchiati, Calle Goldoni, San Marco 4488 (tel: 5285017). Situated close to the Piazza San Marco, this is one of the more expensive hotels which cater for package holidays. Although it lacks the distinctive Venetian character, it is comfortable and well placed for exploring the city.

Cipriani, Giudecca 10 (tel: 5207744). Across the water on the otherwise unfashionable island of Giudecca is the

Cipriani, the caravanserai of the rich and smart. Elegant and comfortable as the former religious institution buildings now are, they lack the character of Venice itself, which lies across the Basin of San Marco and is reached in five minutes by the hotel's free ferry. Its principal asset is its magnificent open-air swimming pool, a miraculous cure for fatigue after a long day's sightseeing in the city. Non-residents lunching at the hotel may be allowed to use the pool if it is not crowded, but the charge is expensive.

Danieli, Riva degli Schiavoni, Castello 4196 (tel: 5226480). Another new hotel building is the bleak modern wing of the Danieli, almost next to the Doges' Palace and overlooking the Basin of San Marco, which makes this hotel the largest in Venice. Guests have included some of the city's most famous visitors – Dickens, Wagner and Proust among them – and the original building has atmosphere and style in its public rooms but is not above catering to the upper end of the package holiday market.

Gabrielli Sandwirth, Riva degli Schiavoni, Castello 4110 (tel: 5231580). This is a former Gothic *palazzo* with its architectural splendours incorporated into its public rooms, courtyard and rose garden; but here, too, single rooms can be cell-sized.

Gritti Palace, Santa Maria del Giglio, San Marco 2467 (tel: 794611). This must be the

Not only the queen of Venetian hotels, but one of the best in Europe – the Gritti Palace stands on the Grand Canal

queen of all the Venetian grand hotels. It was built as a *palazzo* in the 15th century and sumptuously coverted. In summer, its principal delight is the open-air **Terrazza del Doge**, where meals are served beside the Grand Canal. It also rents out furnished apartments for a minimum of one week.

Londra Palace, Riva degli Schiavoni, Castello 4171 (tel: 5200533). This is one of the hotels along the Riva degli Schiavoni – so overlooking the Basin of San Marco. It is efficiently run and comfortable.

Luna, Calle dell' Ascensione, San Marco 1243 (tel: 5289840). Like the Bonvecchiati, this is a

ACCOMMODATION

comfortable package holiday hotel in the higher price bracket. Its position near the Piazza San Marco is convenient for exploring the city.

Metropole, Riva degli Schiavoni, Castello 4199 (tel: 5205044). Another hotel on the Riva degli Schiavoni with a view of the San Marco basin. Comfortable and well run.

Monaco e Grand Canal, Calle Vallaresso, San Marco 1325 (tel: 5200211). Many regular visitors to the grander Venetian hotels now recommend the Monaco e Grand Canal, run by a graduate of Harry's Bar, the famous establishment opposite (see page 77). Like the nearby

The S Cassiano is another converted palazzo – where you can arrive in style at its own watergate

Gritti Palace, it has tables on a terrace beside the Canal Grande and it is only a few steps from the San Marco vaporetto pier. Quiet and cosy, it is also smart and close to the most fashionable shops and the banks.

Moderately-priced Hotels
The following are popular with regular visitors to Venice.

Accademia (tel: 5237846). This is a 17th-century house in its own garden at the junction of two canals, just off the Canal Grande. Only breakfast is served (in the garden when warm). Although the hotel is no longer family owned, the management has improved. Its position remains idyllic, particularly when the wisteria is in bloom, and it is convenient for districts away from the tourist trails. It is prudent to ask for a room

overlooking the front or back garden as those above the canal at one side can be noisy with barges in the early morning.

Flora, Calle Bergamaschi, San Marco 2283/A (tel: 5205844). Some visitors choose the Flora, largely because of its lush, secluded garden and because it is conveniently close to fashionable shops. Some single rooms are rather bleak and cramped.

La Fenice et Des Artistes, Campiello Fenice, San Marco 1936 (tel: 5232333). This hotel is quiet, charmingly furnished and close to the Fenice Theatre.

San Cassiano-Ca' Favretto, Calle della Rosa, Santa Croce 2232 (tel: 721033). Some former patrons of the Accademia have transferred their loyalty to the charming San Cassiano, a 14th-century *palazzo* converted into a hotel a few years ago. On the opposite side of the Grand Canal from the glorious Ca' d'Oro palace, it has its own watergate at which guests can be landed, which is an easier way to arrive than through the maze of alleys ashore. The rooms are comfortable and the staff charming but the stairs are steep (there is no lift), so there are two bedrooms on the ground floor especially for those who cannot manage the ascent.

Seguso, Zattere, Dorsoduro 779 (tel: 5222340). This long-established, family-run hotel is situated on the Zattere, facing across the shipping channel to Giudecca island.

Part of the enjoyment of repeated visits to Venice is in trying different hotels and among those recommended for atmosphere and situation as much as efficiency and convenience are these half-dozen:

Ateneo, San Fantin, San Marco 1876 (tel: 5200588). This quiet hotel, tucked away in a hidden alley, is near the Fenice Theatre, the smart shops and pleasant *campi*.

Bel Sito e Berlino, Santa Maria del Giglio, San Marco 2517 (tel: 5223365). Those wishing to be in the social mainstream but who cannot afford the Gritti Palace choose the Bel Sito, just a short step away and opposite a peculiarly Venetian church with a façade carved with battle rather than Biblical scenes.

Carpaccio, Calle Corner, San Polo 2765 (tel: 523553). On the Grand Canal itself, reached by what is claimed to be the narrowest alley in the city, is the Carpaccio, its long *salone* commanding a wonderful view of water and palaces.

La Residenza, Campo Bandiera e Moro, Castello 3608 (tel: 5285315). This is another palace where the Gritti family lived, hidden away in a *campo* off the Riva degli Schiavoni. This intensely Venetian

La Residenza offers atmosphere at a reasonable price

pensione has a magnificent *salone* on the *piano nobile* with paintings, plasterwork and chandeliers, off which passages lead to comfortable bedrooms. The service is efficient but the management speaks French rather than English to guests.

Pausania, San Barnaba, Dorsoduro 2824 (tel: 5222083). This hotel is on a quiet canal where vegetables are sold to housewives direct from a moored barge. It has recently been modernised but upper-floor bedrooms are reached by a steep stone Gothic staircase in the courtyard.

San Fantin, Campiello Fenice, San Marco 1930/A (tel: 5231401). A quiet hotel, once headquarters for the Venetians' rebellion against Austrian rule in 1848. Its façade is decorated with guns and cannon-balls.

Inexpensive Hotels

The choice of pleasant accommodation for visitors on a low budget is limited, but there are some gems of *pensioni* with historical or literary associations or fine views to compensate for any lack of luxury.

Bucintoro, Riva San Biagio, Castello 2135/A (tel: 5223240). The best view of Venice from any hotel is from here. All the bedroom windows overlook the Riva degli Schiavoni, the Basin of San Marco and the island of San Giorgio, the Salute and the Doges' Palace beyond. Run by a delightful family, it is cosy rather than smart and has its own restaurant, so offering half-board. A century ago it was lodgings for art students, particularly Americans, including James McNeill Whistler who relished the panorama and etched from its windows. Closed mid-November to March 1.

Calcina (tel: 5206466). Another fine view of water – in this case the Canale Giudecca – is from the Calcina, the small hotel on the Zattere, where Ruskin stayed while writing *The Stones of Venice*. Partly modernised and lacking some of its former modest charm, it is a friendly little hotel and a favourite with British visitors. Closed from December to January.

Fiorita, Campiello Nuovo, San Marco 3457/A (tel: 5234754). Among the most simple *pensioni*, the Fiorita is well-sited near the centre, welcoming, clean and uncomplicated; the comfortable rooms have no en suite baths, showers or lavatories but the public ones – which are always kept spotless – are just down the passage.

San Stafano, Campo Francesco Morosini, San Marco 2957 (tel: 5200166). This should not be confused with the similarly named but quite different Casa de' Stefani. It is a small, recently smartened-up hotel, which is situated on the San Marco side of the Accademia bridge.

Lido Hotels
Two gigantic relics of the heyday of the Lido are hotels designed for rich pre-1914 families. Both come alive during the Venice Film Festival which is concentrated on the Lido, and both are as expensive as one would expect from their glamorous associations.

Des Bains, Lungomare Marconi 17 (tel: 5265921). The doom-laden film *Death in Venice* was made here and the hotel exudes a suitably stately gloom. 258 rooms.

Excelsior, Lungomare Marconi 41 (tel: 5260201). This is a turn-of-the-century, mock-Moorish architectural fantasy with 230 rooms, half of them overlooking the sea.

Among the tall trees just inland from the famous beach stands the **Quattro Fontane**, Via 4 Fontane 16 (tel: 5260227), a comfortable, rambling house in an oddly alpine style with a modern wing. In summer, meals and drinks are served in the large garden, and a *vaporetto* stops near by at the Casino pier from lunchtime until 04.00 hours every half hour and takes passengers direct to San Marco.

CULTURE, ENTERTAINMENT, NIGHTLIFE

Venice enjoys a rich cultural life throughout the year. Apart from the Teatro la Fenice (Fenice Theatre), which presents opera in winter and concerts and recitals throughout the year (except August, when it is closed), there are three other theatres: L'Avogaria, Goldoni and Ridotto. Recitals are sometimes held in churches, notably the Pietà, the Ospedaletto and San Stae. There are several cinemas, though films are always shown in Italian. Throughout the year special exhibitions are presented in the principal museums, at the Doges' Palace, on the island of San Giorgio and at the Palazzo Grassi. Often they are advertised with enormous banners in dull Venetian red inscribed in gold and hanging from the bridges over the Grand Canal.

Summer is the season of festivals. The **Biennale** modern art exhibition takes place every other year through the summer, focused on the 40 permanent pavilions in the **Giardini Publici** and galleries around town. The **Festival of Dance** is held in July and the **International Film Festival** is held on the Lido in August and early September.

Venice goes to bed – or at least goes home – early and not long after 22.00 hours, the alleys are quiet except for the occasional footsteps hurrying homeward. A few bars remain open –

notably **A Teatro**, Campo San Fantin, San Marco 1916 (tel: 5221052), which also serves food and sells newspapers and cigarettes; **Haig's Bar**, Campo del Giglio, San Marco 2477 (tel: 5289456), which is near the Gritti Palace Hotel; and **Al Cherubim**, Calle San Antonio, San Marco 4118 (tel: 5238239), near the Rialto – as do those in the grander hotels.

Otherwise most nightlife is to

It's easy to see why Napoleon called Piazza S Marco the most elegant drawing room in Europe

be seen at the casinos, both of
which have their own night-
clubs. On the Canal Grande,
the **Casino Municipale** is in the
Palazzo Vendramin Calergi,
Strada Nuova, Cannaregio 2040
(tel: 710211) and is open from
15.00 to 03.00 hours from
October to March; from April to
September, the **Casino
Municipale**, Lungomare, G
Marconi 4, Lido (tel: 760626) is
open on the Lido during the
same hours, throughout which it
is served by a half-hourly
vaporetto direct from San
Marco after 14.00 hours.

WEATHER AND WHEN TO GO

Spring and autumn are the best
times of year to visit Venice.
From April to June, it is usually
sunny and warm but not stuffy,
although there can be spells of
rain. Early September can still
be very hot and the city
crowded but the second half of
the month and the whole of
October is generally warm and
calm – except for the
occasional thunderstorm – with
sunny days for sightseeing but
without hot, humid nights and

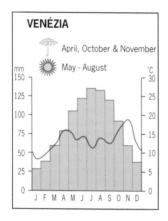

VENÉZIA

April, October & November

May - August

mosquitoes. July and August are the peak holiday months: prices are higher, the city most crowded and the heat such that shade and cool drinks become essentials.

In winter, those hotels remaining open can be busy at Christmas; then again during the *Carnevale*; and finally at Easter, which marks the beginning of the spring season. Venice is at its most empty in November (when many of the hoteliers and restaurateurs take their holidays), early December, January and March. One advantage of an off-peak winter visit is that hotel prices are much reduced. Normally out-of-reach luxury becomes possible on the right package tour. Some prefer it at those quiet times when fog and snow give the city another aspect, just as beautiful but seen through added veils of mystery; or on crisp, cold days when the distant Alps stand out in sharp relief.

HOW TO BE A LOCAL

The best advice is: 'Don't try.' Venetians have always welcomed, or at least accepted, visitors, but only when these have come to live there and can speak Italian can they hope to be considered as 'a local', albeit a foreign one. However, it is fun to share the locals' daily routines of city life and this can easily be done. Take to crossing the Canal Grande by *traghetto* and stand up – as they do – during the brief voyage, even if the gondola rocks in the wake of a *vaporetto*.

Shop in the Rialto markets, the Campo Santa Margherita, or buy fruit and vegetables from the barge moored by the Campo San Barnaba. Try drinking wine in one of the tiny wine-shops in the back alleys, or coffee in the hole-in-the-wall cafés without tables and chairs. Look out for modest *trattorie*, which are crowded with voluble Venetians at lunchtime.

Venetians themselves are formal in their dress – except at carnival-time – and expect visitors to look neat, if not formal, in their city. Beach clothes always look wrong in the city (although not, of course, on the Lido) and are forbidden in most churches. Jackets and ties are expected in the grander hotels and restaurants, although informal clothes are allowed if presentable. It should be noted that formality is expected at the Fenice Theatre.

If you want to eat where the locals do, look out for the popular waterside trattorie

In summer, when it is usually hot, there is much more informality and open-necked shirts are usual wear. In spring and autumn, take light clothes but something warm to wear over them in the evening when it may be chilly. It can rain – occasionally for days on end – particularly in the spring, so be prepared. In winter it can be very cold indeed, and it can snow, so warm clothes and gloves are essential.

The catastrophic high tide, the *acqua alta*, which can flood the city is most likely in late autumn but can occur at other seasons. Duckboard walkways are laid across the Piazza San Marco and other thoroughfares but do not extend throughout the city, so suitable footwear is essential. Some visitors in November and December take rubber waterboots with them, or buy them on arrival; or simple plastic bags which cover the shoes and tie below the knee can be bought there cheaply.

During the February *Carnevale*, those who want to wear fancy dress can buy, or even hire, it in the city if they do not bring it with them. The most elaborate costumes and masks are available in the many shops that now specialise in them but are expensive. The most simple and effective fancy dress is simply a black cloak, a tricon hat and a traditional white mask.

Pigeons might be a favourite with the visitors, but conservationists worry that they may be causing stone erosion

PERSONAL PRIORITIES

Venice is a safe city for women and children. Street crime is rare although burglary is a problem and pickpockets can be expected in crowds at the railway station during the holiday season. Women walking alone at night are seldom pestered, particularly if they maintain a purposeful pace; if they are it is more likely to be by young male visitors to the city than by native Venetians. This is not a problem here as in some Italian cities. Hygienic necessities for women, and baby food and nappies are available in pharmacies as elsewhere in Europe.

CHILDREN

Children are unlikely to be as interested in art and architecture as their elders but there is much in Venice to fascinate them. For a start there is the constant jumping on and off boats, both *vaporetti* and *traghetto* gondolas, and looking out from the tops of the *campanili* of San Marco and San Giorgio. Watching the glass-blowers at work, even at one of the demonstration furnaces in the city, is enthralling and they need no persuading to start collecting little – and cheap – glass animals. Children usually enjoy Italian food, particularly pasta and ice cream, and their presence can enhance a meal, as Italian waiters usually love the under-eights.

Venice is a safe city for children and they can be sent off safely – but preferably not singly – to feed the pigeons in the Piazza San Marco or watch the traffic on the Grand Canal. Some families may prefer to stay on the Lido, where bicycles can be hired and the traffic is sparse and there are sands and sea for swimming. There is a dusty playground in the **Giardini Publici** at the far eastern end of the Riva (*Vaporetto pier*: Giardini).

Behind the Doges' Palace there is the modest **Aquarium** (tel: 5207770) in the Calle degli Albanesi (usually open 09.00 to 17.00 or 21.00 hours but closed on Tuesdays in winter; admission charge), which displays fish from the lagoon as well as the Mediterranean and the tropics.

TIGHT BUDGET

Venice need not be an expensive city. The Venetians' basic transport is free because it is walking; and a large plate of pasta with a glass of wine makes a satisfying cheap meal. Varieties of rolls, brioches and biscuits with coffee can fill the gaps between meals economically.

This is not a city in which to sleep out because not only are its pavements inhospitable and hard but there are very few public lavatories (see page 120). For cheap accommodation enquire at the tourist information offices (*Ente Provinciale per il Turismo*) at Calle Ascensione 71C, Piazza San Marco (tel: 5226356), Santa Lucia railway station (tel: 715016) or at the Piazzale Roma (tel: 5227402). There is a well-run youth hostel, **Ostello Venezia**, Fondamenta delle Zitelle, Giudecca 86 (tel: 5238211) on Giudecca island. There are also a number of religious institutions that offer accommodation (sometimes in a dormitory) and two, **Foresteria Valdese** at Santa Maria Formosa (tel: 5286797), and **Istituto Suaore Canossiane**, Ponte Piccolo, Giudecca 428 (tel: 5222157, women only) are open all the year round. You will find others on a list produced annually by the local tourist organisation; copies are available at the San Marco office.

For recommended inexpensive hotels in the city, see **Accommodation**, page 94.

SPECIAL EVENTS

Winter
In winter the main event is *Carnevale*, which was abolished by the French in 1797 but revived a decade ago with great success. At first largely a Venetian festival, it is now international and, some complain, over-elaborate. For ten days before Lent, masks and fancy dress – which can be bought or hired in the city – are worn all day and most of the night. A daily programme of events includes dancing at night in a *campo*, where mulled wine and traditional sugared cakes are sold from stalls. The exact dates of the *Carnevale* can be had from the Italian State Tourist Office.

Spring
The **Vogalonga** regatta – a 20-mile (32km) rowing race in which anyone can join in any type of oared boat – takes place on the first Sunday after Ascension Day. Boats leave at 09.30 hours from Sant'Elena, at the eastern end of the city. On the same morning, the Mayor and Patriarch of Venice re-enact the ceremony of the **Marriage of Venice with the Sea.** In the old days, the Doge would be rowed out to sea in his ceremonial barge, the *Bucintoro*, and cast a gold wedding ring into the Adriatic, but the occasion is now only a faint echo of the original.

Summer
Cultural events are the **Festival of Dance** in July, the **International Film Festival** on the Lido in August and early

Carnevale has been successfully revived in recent years: festivals and regattas have always been a colourful part of the Venetian calendar

September and, every other year, the **Biennale** modern art exhibition.
The **Festa del Redentore,** which involves the building of a bridge of boats across the Giudecca Canal to the church of the Redentore and was

begun as a festival in thanksgiving for the ending of a plague more than four centuries ago, is held on the third weekend in July.

On the first Sunday in September, the **Regata Storica**, the most spectacular event of the Venetian year, is held. It involves gondola races and a procession up the Grand Canal of boats and barges manned by Venetians in historic costume.

Autumn

The opera season opens at the Teatro la Fenice in November. Important art exhibitions and a Festival of Contemporary Music are held.

On 21 November the **Festa della Madonna della Salute** – a procession across the Grand Canal on floating bridges to the church of the Salute to give thanks for the ending of another plague in the 17th century – takes place.

On a hot summer day, where better than the beach? However, many are private and charge a fee

SPORT

Other than the regattas for gondoliers and watermen, there is little sport in Venice itself although there is a stadium on the Isola di Sant'Elena at the extreme eastern tip of the city. Sporting activity is largely confined to the Lido. There are the Lido Tennis Club, 163 Via San Gallo (tel: 760954) and the Tennis Union, Via Fausta (tel: 968134) and the major hotels have their own courts. Also on the island is the Venice Riding Club (*Circolo Ippico Veneziano*, tel: 765162), and the Excelsior Hotel offers sailing in summer.

Swimming

The Lido is the bathing-place of Venice but much of its seven-mile (11km) beach are owned by hotels or bathing establishments, and a hefty fee is payable on each stretch for changing facilities and deck chairs. The hire of beach huts is particularly expensive.

The only public swimming pool in Venice is that at the Hotel Cipriani and that is reserved for those staying, or buying expensive non-residents' tickets.

There are good bathing beaches on the mainland east of Venice between the landing-stage at Punta Sabbioni (Ferry No 14 from San Zaccaria or the Lido) and Lido di Jesolo, which is connected to Venice by a bus service from the Piazzale Roma.

DIRECTORY

Contents

Arriving
Camping
Crime
Customs Regulations
Departures
Driving
Electricity
Embassies and
  Consulates
Emergency
  Telephone
  Numbers

Entertainment
  Information
Etiquette
Getting About
Health
Holidays
Lost Property
Media
Money Matters
Opening Times
Personal Safety
Pharmacist

Places of Worship
Police
Post Office
Senior Citizens
Students and
  Youths
Telephones
Time
Tipping
Toilets
Tourist Offices
Travel Agencies

Arriving

By Air

The easiest way to visit Venice is on a package holiday, when you will be taken to your hotel from the airport and back again, often using a water-taxi at no extra charge.

The independent traveller will arrive at **Marco Polo Airport** on the mainland at Tessera, eight miles (13km) to the north of Venice. (**Treviso** airport, 19 miles/30km north of Venice, is sometimes used by charter flights). It is also convenient for the whole of the Veneto and the Dolomites. There is no airport tax payable at either of the Venetian airports.

Public water-buses ply between the airport and San Marco in the centre of the city and the half-hour journey can also be made by the much more expensive water-taxi. If choosing the latter, you should always agree to a fare with the driver before embarking. Buses run every hour between the airport and the Piazzale

Roma, the road traffic terminus at the Venice end of the causeway across the lagoon, and fares are cheap; the ACTV No 5 bus is the one to look out for. Taxis are also available for this 30-minute journey.

For those arriving at Treviso airport, a coach link into Venice is provided by many air charter companies; otherwise take the No 6 bus from outside the arrivals building into Treviso, from where there are regular coach and train connections with Venice.

By Rail

A pleasant way to travel is by rail. Throughout the year services from London to Paris (via the ferry from Dover or Folkestone to Calais or Boulogne) link with overnight trains – with sleeping-cars – to Venice, including *The Galilei* and the Paris-Venezia Express. During the summer holiday season, through 'car-sleeper' trains run from Boulogne to Milan and Bologna from where you can continue your journey to Venice by car.

The most luxurious means of travel is by the Venice Simplon-Orient Express direct from London to Venice. This runs from the end of February to mid-November and, although the journey is very expensive, the train's luxurious coaches and sumptuous food make it far more than a mere means of transport.

Arrivals by rail are at the Stazione Santa Lucia at the western end of the Grand Canal and there are several *vaporetto* (water-bus) stops immediately outside the station.

By Car and Coach

The route over the Alps is the shortest, but can be quite arduous; most drivers make for the south of France then head east into northern Italy. French Railways run an overnight Motorail service in summer between Calais and Innsbruck, arriving at the latter in early morning so that Venice can be reached via the Brenner Pass in a drive of less than five hours with the option of stopping for lunch by Lake Garda or in Vicenza.

From the *autostrada* (motorway) the exit for Venice (Venezia) is 'Mestre', and a roadbridge leads to Venice. In Venice, see **Driving (Parking)**. Travellers by coach are set down at the Piazzale Roma, which is also well-served by *vaporetti*. Motorists leave their cars at the *tronchetto* (car park) at the end of the causeway and pay the parking charge on departure; this is served by the Nos 1, 8, 28 and 34 *vaporetti*.

By Sea

Those arriving by sea will land either in the docks at the western end of the city, or at the eastern end of the Riva degli Schiavoni, both close to *vaporetto* piers.

Entry Formalities

British residents need only a valid full passport, or a British Visitors' Passport, to enter Italy. Citizens of Eire, the US, Canada, Australia and New Zealand require only a passport for stays of up to three months.

Camping

Camping sites nearest Venice on the mainland are situated on the outskirts of Mestre and Marghera, near the Marco Polo airport, at Tessera and at Fusina.

More attractive (and more expensive) are the numerous camping sites along the coast from Punta Sabbioni to Jésolo, on the mainland north of the Lido. The **Marina di Venezia** at Via Montello 6 (tel: 966146), and **Miramare** at Lungomare Dante Alighieri 29 (tel: 966150), both open from April to September, and can be reached by *vaporetto* route 14, from Riva degli Schiavoni to Punta, stopping close to both sites.

Chemist see Pharmacist

Crime

The streets of Venice are among the safest in Italy. But keep an eye on your luggage when waiting at the airport, railway station or bus terminus. Hotel bedroom doors – and windows within climbing distance of the ground – should be kept locked in your absence.

Customs Regulations

Since 1 January 1993 there are no restrictions on allowances for EC residents on goods bought in the EC that are for your own use, although guide limits by Customs are as follows:
800 cigarettes, 400 cigarillos, 200 cigars, 10 litres of spirits, 20 litres of fortified wine, 90 litres of wine, 110 litres of beer. For non-EC residents the following allowances apply: 200 cigarettes *or* 100 cigarillos *or* 50 cigars *or* 250 grams of tobacco; 1 litre of spirits or

One of the classic Venetian views: looking towards San Giorgio island from the Campanile di San Marco

DIRECTORY

Slav merchants unloaded their ships here; today Riva degli Schiavoni is crowded with cafés and stalls

strong liqueurs *or* 2 litres of fortified or sparkling wine, or low strength liqueurs *plus* 2 litres of still table wine; 50 grams of perfume or 250cc/ml of toilet water; other goods to the value of £36. For goods exceeding this value an application to export must be presented to Customs.

In addition, items for *personal use* may be temporarily imported into Italy free of duty but take receipts for valuable articles to avoid paying duty on them.

Currency

Visitors may import an unlimited amount of Italian or foreign currency, and export up to 1,000,000 *lire* and up to the equivalent of 5,000,000 *lire* in foreign currency. If amounts in excess of this are to be exported, the amount must be declared upon entry using the form V2, which must be shown to Customs when leaving Italy. Since there are frequent variations in the amounts of

Wagons-Lits/Cook, Piazzetta
Leonici, San Marco 289 (tel:
5223405)
American Express, San Moisè,
San Marco 1471 (tel: 5200844)

Driving (Parking)

Though Venice is connected to
the mainland by roadbridge, no
road communications exist in
the city itself. Drivers have to
leave their vehicles in multi-
storey garages or open-air car
parks at the island end of the
bridge (unless going to the
Lido, in which case you take the
car ferry from Tronchetto).
Automatic signs on motorway
approaches indicate available
space at car parks. Parking is
limited, especially in summer.
Car parks at Piazzale Roma are
the most convenient, with a
vaporetto landing stage and
taxi-stand. The municipal car
park (*Autorimessa Comunale di
Venezia*), situated at the end of
the bridge, is the most
reasonably priced. Do not be
tempted to park outside in
Piazzale Roma as cars that do
so will be towed away.
Otherwise there is parking at
ever-expanding Tronchetto
with good *vaporetto* services to
the centre of Venice.
Car parking charges vary
according to the time of year,
length of stay and size of
vehicle, but it is never cheap.
The open-air parking spaces
are less expensive than the new
multi-storey parking and just as
secure. If car parks are full, or
you refuse to pay exorbitant
parking fees, you can leave
your vehicle on the mainland in
Mestre or Marghera, and
continue your journey by

currency allowed in or out of
Italy, the latest regulations
should be checked before
departure.

Departures

The following telephone
numbers may be useful:
Marco Polo Airport – tel:
661111
State Railways – tel: 715555

Airlines

British Airways – tel:
5285026/5205699
Alitalia – tel: 5200355/5225428

Ticket agencies

CIT, Piazza San Marco, San
Marco 4850 (tel: 5285480)

Paintings by Tintoretto adorn the ceiling of the Sala del Senato in the Palazzo Ducale

frequent bus and train services to Venice.

Electricity

The supply is 220 volts AC (50 cycles), though any British, Australian or New Zealand appliances normally requiring a slightly higher voltage, will work. For visitors from the US or Canada with appliances normally requiring 100/120 volts, and not fitted for dual-voltage, a voltage transformer is required.

Plugs are the continental two round-pin type, so an electrical adaptor is useful, best brought with you from home.

Embassies and Consulates

British Consulate, Palazzo Querini, Dorsoduro 1051. Found near the Accademia Bridge (tel: 5227207). Eire, the US, Canada, Australia and New Zealand do not maintain consulates in the city

and help must be sought from their embassies or consulates in Rome:
Eire (tel: 06-6782541)
United States (tel: 06-46741)
Canada (tel: 06-8415341)
Australia (tel: 06-832721 and 06-841241)
New Zealand (tel: 06-851225)

Emergency Telephone Numbers

Dial 113 on any telephone (free of charge) and ask for the police, ambulance or fire service. Alternatively, dialling 112 puts you straight through to the *Carabinieri* (police); 115 to the *Vigili del Fuoco* (fire brigade) and dial 523000 for an ambulance (see Italian phrases, page 123).

Two hospitals have casualty departments: the **Ospedale Civile** in Santi Giovanni e Paolo (tel: 784516); and on the Lido, the **Ospedale al Mare**, Lungomare d'Annunzio (tel: 5261750).

Visitors in need of assistance can call the Venice Police Headquarters (Aliens and Passport Office) on 5203222.

Entertainment Information

Local papers, the *Gazzettino* and *Nuova Venezia* contain up-to-the-minute schedules for theatres, cinemas and other forms of entertainment. The free Italian/English publication *Un Ospite di Venezia*, contains a good listings section, while the cost-conscious *Venezia in Jeans* is useful for the young. Tourist Information Offices are another source of help, and San Marco APT (tel: 5298730 or 5226356) is the best for information about cultural and other events.

Etiquette

To avoid offence, visitors should behave appropriately when visiting churches: do not walk round during services. Do not enter wearing beach clothes; men should remove their hats. If the sacristan has been helpful with explanations or turning on lights, a small tip is appropriate. On leaving, a modest donation to the offertory box is appreciated.

Getting About

There are two ways of getting about Venice: by water or on foot.

By *Vaporetto*

The *vaporetto* is the principal means of transport and a study of routes and timetables at any pier is an early essential. Vaporetto stops are shown on the maps on pages 18-19 and 24-25. *Vaporetti* are operated by the public transport system, ACTV. Line (*Linea*) No 1 runs from the *tronchetto*, along the length of the Grand Canal, down the Riva degli Schiavoni and across to the Lido. Otherwise the re-routing and re-numbering of the ferries began at the end of 1993 and is expected to continue for some time. Route No 2, linking the transport termini with the main piers on the Grand Canal and Giudecca island has been re-numbered No 82, while No 5, which crosses to the island of Murano is now numbered No 52. Changes in routing will continue, and extra ferries come into service for the summer, but the latest timetables are displayed on the piers, or call ACTV (tel:

DIRECTORY

5287886).

Rather than buy a ticket for each journey at a ticket office on the pier (if there is one), or pay more for a ticket on board, opt for one of several alternatives. If it is planned to make six or more journeys in 24 hours, buy a 24-hour ticket (*biglietto turistico*); or if at least 10 journeys are planned within three days, buy a 72-hour ticket; or buy a *blocchetta* of 10 or more tickets to be used over any period.

The identity card (*carta Venezia*) which allows half-price fares, is for residents only and is obtainable at the ACTV office at Piazzale Roma. But remember that tickets must be date-stamped by the automatic machine on each pier before first use. There is a supplementary charge – usually another full fare – for baggage other than hand-luggage.

By Water-taxi

Water-taxi speedboats ply for hire at the airport, railway station, the Piazzale Roma and San Marco and can be ordered by telephone (tel: 5232326 or 5222303). They are expensive and although fares are regulated by a tariff it is prudent to agree to the price when ordering; better still, do so through either the tour operator's courier or the hotel's hall porter or receptionist.

By Gondola

The hire of a gondola – the most enjoyable means of transport in the city – is expensive, although obviously less so when the cost is split between several passengers. Fares are governed by a tariff and should be about 70,000 *lire* for a 50-minute trip, with a surcharge for night trips, but it is often easiest to establish terms by ordering a gondola through the tour operator's courier or the hotel staff. As an extravagant but memorable outing, it is worth getting a party together to share the cost of a two-hour gondola-ride down the Grand Canal with a picnic supper on board.

Don't look down your nose at the cruises by flotillas of gondolas packed with tourists and entertained by singers, those after dark marketed as a 'Moonlight Serenade'. This is a good way of seeing the Grand Canal and the secretive lesser canals from a gondola and is not expensive.

Ferry gondolas – *traghetti* – ply to and fro across the Grand Canal between special piers at half a dozen crossing-points and are used by tourists and Venetians, (the latter tend to stand throughout the short voyage). The very reasonable fare is paid to the gondolier.

On Foot

Most movement in the city is, of course, on foot and the first essential is to buy a reliable map. Partly because many alleys pass underneath buildings there are no wholly accurate maps of the city but it is worth looking for a reputable map-publisher (such as Hallwag, Kummerly and Frey, Falk, FMB and LAC). Sooner or later, everyone gets a little lost in Venice before again sighting one of the yellow signs painted on the corners of buildings giving directions to the main destinations: *Per San Marco; Per Rialto; Per Ferrovia* (railway station) and so on. Above all, pack a comfortable pair of walking shoes and, unless your hotel is on, or very near, one of the main canals, bring luggage that can be carried easily, or use a folding trolley.

Health

No inoculation certificates are required for your stay. However, it is advisable to wash all fruit and vegetables. Venice's tap water is perfectly safe to drink as is the water from drinking fountains around the city. In cases where the water is not safe to drink it will be marked with a sign – *acqua non potabile*. Nationals of the European Community can take advantage of Italy's health services under the same terms as residents of the country. If you are British you will need form E111 (available from your local Department of Health before you leave). If you need treatment, go to the local Health Unit (*Unità Sanitoria Locale/USL*), the local tourist office should be able to give you the address. There you will be given a certificate of entitlement. Ask to see a list of the scheme's doctors and dentists. Take the certificate to any doctor or dentist on the list and you will

Watch the sights of Venice slide past from the comfort of a gondola – the traditional way to travel

The dramatic octagonal nave of Salute has seven altars as well as sculpture and paintings

be treated free of charge, though you must pay 25 per cent of the cost of a prosthesis. Also, private medical schemes give full cover during your stay. If your ailment is a minor one, chemists (*farmacia*) can give advice and dispense prescriptions (see **Pharmacist**). The high cost of medical treatment makes travel insurance **essential** if you are a **non-EC citizen.** For medical treatment and medicines, keep all bills to claim the money back later.
Travel insurance however, is advisable for all in the event of any kind of emergency (see also, **Emergency Telephone Numbers**).

Holidays
Shops, offices and schools are closed (but some bars and restaurants stay open) on New Year's Day, Epiphany (6 January), Liberation Day (25 April), Easter Monday, Labour Day (1 May), Assumption Day (15 August), All Saints' Day (1 November), Conception Day (8 December), Christmas Day and St Stephen's Day, or Boxing Day (26 December). Many shops and offices work shorter hours for the local festival, Festa della Salute (21 November).

Lost Property
Enquire at the City Hall (*Municipio*) for property lost in Venice itself (tel: 5208844); at Santa Lucia station for anything lost on trains or stations (tel: 716122, ex 3238); and for property left on *vaporetti*, enquire of ACTV, the operators (tel: 780310). For items mislaid at the Marco Polo airport, telephone 661266 for information.

Media

Literature

Local newspapers are the *Il Gazzettino* and *Nuova Venezia* (good for listings).

The weekly *Un Ospite di Venezia* ('A Guest in Venice'), is free and is available through information offices, agencies and hotels, and gives up-to-date information to the visitor. English-language newspapers can be found at the railway station, by the Calle dell' Ascensione post office and various newsstands throughout the city – usually a day or two late.

Television

There are three state-run channels, *RAI 1, 2*, and *3*, serving up heavy helpings of American sitcoms and films as well as uninspiring Italian cabaret shows, but with some good news reportage programmes.

Radio

The *RAI* channels, mostly provide daytime listening of non-stop dance music. The FM waves are crowded with other stations, mostly pop music again. If you want news, tune into the BBC World Service.

Money Matters

The currency is the Italian *lira* (plural *lire*); you will find it abbreviated to '*L*' in shops. The coins that are most frequently encountered are 100, 200 and 500 *lire*; smaller denomination coins (5, 10 and 20 *lire*) may sometimes be given in change. Notes appear in values of 1,000, 2,000, 5,000, 10,000, 50,000 and 100,000 *lire*. (For details on the importation and exportation of currency, refer to **Customs Regulations**.)

Travellers' cheques are the safest way to carry money. You usually, though not always, pay a small commission when you exchange them for *lire*. With the Eurocheque card you can get cash from virtually all banks in Venice. Major credit cards such as Visa and American Express are accepted in many hotels and shops and some restaurants, though Access (Mastercard) is not as widely accepted.

Banks

These are concentrated in two main areas – Campo San Bartolomeo (near the Rialto bridge) and Calle Larga XXII Marzo (near the Piazza). There is not much to choose between them in terms of commission and exchange rates. (For hours, see **Opening Times**.) The American Express office in Salizzada San Moisè, is useful for exchange dealings out of office hours; it is open 08.00-20.00 hours, Monday to Saturday.

There are exchange bureaux (*cambio*) wherever tourists gather. Open all week until late at night, they are useful in emergencies but their rates can be steep; the same can be said of exchange desks in hotels.

Opening Times

Banks

Monday to Friday from 08.30 to 13.30 hours and again from 15.00 to 16.00 hours.

DIRECTORY

Churches
Most open around 07.00/08.00 hours until noon, opening again at 15.00/16.00 hours until 18.00/19.00 hours.
Where possible, churches appearing in the **What To See** section are credited with specific times.

Museums and Galleries
These usually close on public holidays, and on other holidays are only open in the morning. Refer to individual museums in the **What To See** section for specific times of opening.

Post Offices
The main office at Fondaco dei Tedeschi is open Monday to Saturday from 08.15 to 19.00 hours.
Branch offices open Monday to Friday from 08.10 to 13.25 hours, and Saturday until noon.

Shops and Most Businesses
Monday to Saturday from 08.00/09.00 to 13.00 hours and again from 16.00 to 19.00/20.00 hours.

Personal Safety
Visitors should exercise normal care of themselves and their property in Venice, although crime is not a great problem. Documents and spare money should be left in the hotel safe. See also **Personal Priorities** page 100.

Pharmacist
A rota system ensures that there is always a chemist open somewhere in the city. Every *farmacia* should display the address of the nearest night chemist on its door. A list also appears in the local

newspaper, or you can ring 192 for information.

Places of Worship
Roman Catholic services are held regularly in most of the churches of Venice and their times are advertised at the door. High Mass is celebrated at the Basilica of San Marco at 10.00 hours and the Gregorian chant sung in the church of San Giorgio Maggiore on the island of San Giorgio at 10.30 hours. Confessions are heard in English on Sundays (07.00 to 10.00 hours) at San Marco and several other churches. Details from the Diocesan Tourist Office, Piazzale Roma 469a. Anglican services are held in the Church of St George in the Campo San Vio on Sundays (*Vaporetto*: Accademia or Salute).

Police
The state police (*Questura*) have their headquarters on the Fondamenta San Lorenzo. For tourists in difficulty they have a special Aliens and Passport Office (tel: 5203222).
The Venice City Police (*Vigili Urbani*) have their headquarters in the Palazzo Loredan in the City Hall (*Municipo*): they can be contacted on 5224063.
The *Carabinieri* (the armed police) should only be contacted in an emergency (tel: 112).

Post Office
The main post office is at Fondaco dei Tedeschi, near the Rialto Bridge (tel: 5220606), with telephone exchange and telegraph and telex office. Any poste restante (*ferma posta*) can be collected Monday to

*Murano glass is still some of the
world's finest – but be selective*

Saturday from 08.15 to 13.45
hours, with passport evidence.
The principal branch offices are
in Calle dell'Ascensione
(western end of Piazza San
Marco) and at Zattere. (For
times, see **Opening Times**).
Stamps can also be bought in
tabacchi and in some gift shops.
Postal addresses in Venice are
simply the name of the *sestiere*
(district) and a number, so are
intelligible only to postmen and
no help with finding a
destination. This is usually
preceded by the name of the
campo or *calle* but even then the
numbered door can be difficult
to find for the uninitiated
stranger.

Senior Citizens
British citizens over the age of
60 are admitted free to state-
owned museums and
monuments. Citizens of other
countries should check with
ENIT to find out whether such
concessions exist for them.

Students and Youths
Visitors between the ages of
14 and 30 qualify for the
discount scheme known as
'Rolling Venice'. For a fee of
5,000 Lira it entitles you to
discounts on 25 museums and
galleries, 72-hour *vaporetto*
tickets, as well as savings at
restaurants, hotels and in
shops (you are provided with
a useful little guide to the city
when paying your fee, and
recoup the initial cost almost

immediately by visiting some of the 'big' sights). The scheme operates during the summer or *Carnevale*.

Enrol at offices in the railway station or in the office at the back of the Piazza, directions can be sought at the main tourist information office (look for the sign *Alla Gioventù* rather than Rolling Venice).

Telephones

Public telephones usually have clear written instructions in English. They take 100, 200 or 500 *lire* coins, or tokens (*gettone*) valued at 200 *lire*, or phone cards (*schede telefóniche*) which can be bought from *SIP* offices (the state telephone company) or *tabacchi*, bars and news stands. International calls can be made from public callboxes marked *interurbano*. From the two main *SIP* offices at Piazzale Roma and in the main post office at Rialto you can dial direct and be charged afterwards. Hotels will also perform this service but normally charge 25 per cent more.

The Grand Canal, known to locals as the Canalazzo, is timeless – only means of transport have changed

For international calls dial the international and country code (given below), the area code (minus the first '0'), then the number.
UK: 00 44
Eire: 00 353
US: 00 1
Canada: 00 1
Australia: 00 61
New Zealand: 00 64
When telephoning Venice from outside the city, the code prefix is 041.

Useful Phone Numbers:
Tourist Information (San Marco): 5226356
Flight Information (Marco Polo Airport): 661111
Train Information: 715555
Public Transport (ACTV): 5287886
Post Office and Telegraph Services: 5220606 and 5285949

Time
Local standard time is one hour ahead of Greenwich Mean Time. Italian Summer Time (when clocks go forward an hour) is in operation from the last weekend of March to the last weekend of September. The time is one hour ahead of Britain except for a few weeks from late September to late October when the time is the same. Local time is also 6 hours ahead of New York time, 9 hours behind time in Sydney and 11 hours behind New Zealand time for most of the year.

Tipping
In hotels service charges are included in the rates, but tip for extra services as elsewhere. In restaurants, where a service charge is included in the bill, add an extra 1,000 *lire* a head for the waiter, or a little more for exceptional attention. In cinemas and theatres, an usherette taking you to your seat will expect a tip. Five hundred *lire* is the minimum that should be given for any service.

Toilets
As was demonstrated when vast crowds converged on Venice for the disastrous pop concert in 1989, public lavatories are scarce in Venice and are usually shut at night.

DIRECTORY

They are to be found (but not always open) at Santa Lucia railway station; the Piazzale Roma; in Campo San Bartolomeo, near the Rialto; opposite the arcades at the western end of the Piazza San Marco; and beneath the western end of the Accademia Bridge. A small fee is payable at each. There is also a men's urinal in the Campo San Polo. Otherwise the larger bars have *toilette*, which can be visited at the cost of a drink, remembering not to confuse the signs *Signori* (Men) and *Signore* (Women). The other word for WC is *gabinetto*.

Tourist Offices

The Italian State Tourist Office (ENIT) can help with information on Venice before you go.

UK

1 Princes Street
London W1R 8AY
(tel: 071-408-1254; after 16 April 1995, tel: 0171-408–1254)

Eire

47 Merrion Square
Dublin 2
(tel: 0001-676 6397)

US

630 Fifth Avenue
Suite 1565 New York 10111
(tel: 212-245 4822/314)

Canada

1 Place Ville Marie
Suite 1914
Montreal
Quebec H3B 3M9
(tel: 514-866-7667/8/9)

Australia and New Zealand

c/o Alitalia
Orient Overseas Buildings,
Suite 202, 32 Bridge Street,
Sydney
New South Wales
(tel: 02-271308)

In Venice, *Ente Provinciale per il Turismo* (EPT) or *Azienda di Promozione Turistica* (APT) can provide practical information on the city. Information offices are to be found at:
Calle Ascensione 71c,
San Marco
(tel: 5226356). Open 08.30 to 19.00 hours Monday to Saturday, with shorter winter hours.
Piazzale Roma 504d
(tel: 5227404).
Open 08.00 to 20.00 hours, summer only.
Viale Santa Maria Elisabetta, Lido
(tel: 5265721).
Open 09.00 to 14.00 hours Monday to Saturday.
Stazione Santa Lucia
(tel: 719078).
Open 08.00 to 20.00 hours.
Autostrada (Motorway)
at Marghera
(tel: 937764).

Travel Agencies

American Express,
Salizzada San Moisè,
San Marco 1474
(tel: 5200844)
useful for help and advice.
CIT, Piazza San Marco 48/50
(tel: 5285480)
Wagons-Lits/Cook,
Piazzetta dei Leoncini,
San Marco 289-305
(tel: 5223405).

LANGUAGE

Venetians are delighted when a foreign visitor tries to speak to them in Italian. But those who speak the language moderately well should not attempt to imitate the Venetian dialect, as this might be thought patronising

Pronunciation

The words most often mis-pronounced are those including single or double *c*s or *g*s. A single *c* or *g* is soft (as in *c*hild, or *g*entleman) before an *e* or *i*, but hard (as in *c*ap or *g*old) before an *a*, *o* or *u*. Both a double *cc* or a double *gg* is soft before an *e* or *i*, while a *ch* or *gh* is hard. In words including *qu*, the *u* is pronounced as in *squ*at, but the *g* in *gl* or *gn* is not pronounced (as in ta*gl*iatelle and si*gn*or).

A Venetian Glossary

acqua alta a high tide that floods Venice
basilica cathedral
calle pedestrian alley
campanile bell-tower
campiello small square
campo square
casa, or **ca'** a large house or *palazzo*
cortile courtyard
fondamente waterside promenade
molo quay
palazzo palace
piano nobile principal floor
rio terra filled-in canal, now a wide *calle*
riva wide waterside promenade
salone principal reception room of *palazzo*

Four stone emperors, carved in the 4th century, now guard the Palazzo Ducale

The skills, and licence, of the gondolier pass from father to son

sandolo Venetian skiff
scuola building used for community welfare and charity
Serenissima the title 'Most Serene One' referring to Venice
sestiere a district of Venice
sottoportago a *calle* running through a building, or along an arcade
squero boat-builders' yard
traghetto ferry gondola
vaporetto Venetian waterbus

Basic Vocabulary
yes si
no no
please per favore
thank you grazie
I beg your pardon scusi
that's all right va bene

excuse me permesso
not at all/don't mention it prego
can I help you? posso aiutaria?
hello, or goodbye ciao
hello (on the telephone) pronto
good morning buon giorno
good afternoon/evening buona sera
good night buona notte
today oggi
tomorrow domani
morning mattino
afternoon pommeriggio
evening sera
night notte
day giorno
week settimana
month mese
year anno
hour ora
early presto, di buon'ora
late ultimo, scorso

large grande
small piccolo, -a
hot caldo, -a
cold freddo, -a
good buono, -a
bad cattivo, -a
open aperto
shut chiuso
entrance entrata
exit uscita
all tutto
many/much molto
why? perchè?
when? quando?
what? cosa?
where? dove?
upstairs sopra
downstairs da basso
inside dentro
expensive caro
cheap a buon mercato
right destra
left sinistra
come in! avanti!

Phrases
I do not understand non la capisco
do you speak English? parla l'Inglese?
I cannot speak Italian non parlo l'Italiano
please speak slowly parli adagio, la prego
what do you want? cosa desidera?
what is the matter? cosa c'è?
where are we going? dove andiamo?
I shall stay here restero qui
is there a doctor near by? c'è un dottore qui vicino?
call a policeman at once chiami presto un vigile
I am feeling very ill mi sento molto male

At the Hotel
can you give me a room for the night? mi può dare una camera per la notte?
what is the price of a room for each day? quanto costa al giorno una camera?
I do not like this room non mi piace questa camera
have you no cheaper room? non ne ha una che costa meno?

In the Restaurant
can we lunch here? si può fare colazione qui?
have you a table for …? avete un tavolo per …?
we do not want a full meal non desideriamo un pasto completo
may we have another table? portremmo spostarci?
where is the washroom? dov'è la toiletta?
please may I have the menu? cia dia la carta, per piacere?
the bill, please il conto, per favore

Food
lamb agnello
hors d'oeuvres antipasto
roast meat arrosto
boiled meats bollito misto
game cacciagione
meat carne
cauliflower cavolfiore
cabbage cavolo
onion cipolle
rabbit coniglio
raw crudo
sweets dolci
strong, black coffee espresso
liver fegato
flat pasta fettuccine
figs fichi
cheese formaggio
omelette frittata
fried fritto
fruit frutta
shellfish frutti di mare
mushrooms funghi
prawns gamberi

LANGUAGE

ice-cream gelato
grilled griglia (alla)
salad insalata
lemon limone
fruit salad macedonia di frutta
pork maiale
beef manzo
jam marmellata
apple mela
honey miele
soup minestra
nuts noci
veal knuckle osso bucco
oysters ostriche
bread roll panino
cream panna
potatoes patate
pear pera
peach pesca
fish pesce
peas piselli
chicken pollo
tomato pomodoro
grapefruit pompelmo
ham prosciutto
plums prugne
rice riso
sausage salsiccia
sardines sarde
escalopes scaloppine
sole sogliola
spinach spinaci
sugar sugo
sandwich tramezzino
eggs uova
grapes uva
green vegetables verdure
veal vitello
courgettes zucchini
soup zuppa

Drink
mineral water acqua minerale
beer birra
fruit juice succa di frutta
milk latte
coffee caffè
tea tè
chocolate cioccolato

cold freddo
hot caldo
glass bicchiere
bottle bottiglia
half-bottle mezzo bottiglia
dry secco
sweet dolce

Transport
airport aeroporto
bus autobus
seaport porto
motorboat motoscafo
train treno
ticket biglietto
single andata
return andata e ritorno
first/second class
prima/seconda classe
station stazione
sleeping berth cuccetta

Shops
bank banca
bookshop libreria
butcher macelleria
chemist farmacia
cleaner tintoria
fishmonger pescheria
greengrocer ortolano
grocer drogheria
hairdresser parucchiere, -a
market mercato
optician ottico
post office ufficio postale
stationer cartoleria
tailor sarto
tourist bureau ente del turismo
travel agent agenzia di viaggio

Numbers
one uno, una
two due
three tre
four quattro
five cinque
six sei
seven sette
eight otto
nine nove

Stand like Byron's Childe Harold on the Ponte dei Sospiri, with 'a palace and prison on either hand'. The famous stone bridge dates from the early 17th century

ten dieci
first primo
second secondo
third terzo

Days of the Week
Sunday domenica
Monday lunedi
Tuesday martedi
Wednesday mercoledi
Thursday giovedi
Friday venerdi
Saturday sabato

Months of the Year
January gennaio
February febbraio
March marzo
April aprile
May maggio
June giugnio
July luglio
August agosto
September settembre
October ottobre
November novembre
December dicembre

Seasons
spring primavera
summer estate
autumn autunno
winter inverno

INDEX

INDEX

The index lists both English and Italian place names

Accademia 50–1
accommodation 89–95, 101
air travel 105, 109
Angelo Raffaele 33
Archaeological Museum 55
architecture 11–13
Arsenale 46–7
art 13–14
Asolo 65

banks 115
bars 82–3, 96
Basilica di San Marco 29–30
Bassano del Grappa 66
Belluno 66
birdlife 69–70, 71–2, 73, 74–5, 76
Bridge of Sighs 27, 125
budget tips 101
Burano 15, 58–9
buses 105

Ca' Barbaro 20
Ca' Mocenigo 20
Ca' d'Oro Galleria Franchetti 51–2
Ca' Pesaro Galleria d'Arte Moderna e Museo Orientale 52–3
Ca' Rezzonico Museo del Settecento Veneziano 53
cafés 81–2
Campanile di San Marco 30–1
camping 106
Campo San Barnaba 23
Campo San Polo 23
Campo Santa Margherita 23
Campo Santa Maria Formosa 23
Campo Santi Giovanni e Paolo 23

Canal Grande 4, 17–21, 118
  map 24–5
Carmini 33
Carnevale 10, 100, 102
Casa Goldoni 53
casinos 96–7
chemists 116
children's entertainment 101
Chioggia 59
churches 29–46, 116
climate 97–8
Clock Tower 49
coach travel 106
Collezione (Racolta) Guggenheim 54
Correr Museum 55
Cortina 66
culinary specialities 77
cultural events 96
currency 108–9, 115
Customs House 47–8
customs regulations 107–8

districts of Venice 14–15
  map 18–19
Dogana di Mare 47–8
Doges' Palace 12, 25–7, 110, 121
dress 98–100
driving 109–10
driving to Venice 106
Duomo (Chioggia) 59

embassies and consulates 110–11
emergencies 111
entertainment and nightlife 96–7, 111
environmental problems 11

festivals and events 96, 102–3
Fondamenta delle Zattere 22
food and drink 77–83, 88
Foresta Tarvisio 75
Fortress of Sant' Andrea 60
Fortuny Museum 55

Franchetti Gallery 51–2
Fusine Natural Park 75

Gallery of Modern Art and Oriental Museum 52–3
Gesuati 33
Gesuiti 34
Ghetto 22-3
Giardini 22
Giglio 35
Goldoni Museum 53
gondolas 112
Grand Canal 4, 17–21, 118,
  map 24–5
Guggenheim Collection 54

Harry's Bar 78, 83
health matters 113–14
history of Venice 8–11
hotels 89–95

Italian Alps 75–6
Laguna Veneta 14–15, 69
  map 58
language 121–5
Lido 59–60
Lido di Jésolo 68
Lipica 66
local etiquette 98, 111
local time 119
lost property 114–15

Madonna dell' Orto 35
maps
  districts 18–19
  excursions from Venice 67
  Grand Canal 24–5
  Italy 4
  Laguna Veneta 58
markets 88
medical treatment 113–14
Miracoli 35
Mocenigo Palace 56–7
money 108–9, 115
Monte Grappa 66
Monti del Sole 75
Murano 60, 61–2, 84, 117

Museo Archeologico 55

Museo Correr 55

Museo di Storia Naturale 56

Museo Fortuny 55

Museo Querini-Stampalia 55–6

Museo Storico Navale 56

Museo Vetrario di Murano 61

Museum of 18th-century Venice 53

museums and galleries 50–7, 116

Natural History Museum 56

Naval Museum 56

newspapers 111, 115

opening times 115

Ospedaletto 35

Padova 64–5

Padua(Padova) 64–5

palaces 25–8

Palazzo Contarini 28

Palazzo Ducale 12, 25–7, 110, 121

Palazzo Grassi 27

Palazzo Labia 27–8

Palazzo Mocenigo 56–7

Parco Naturale Adamello-Brenta 75

Parco Naturale di Fusine 75

Parco Naturale Panveggio-Pale di San Martino 75

parking 109–10

passports 106

personal safety 100, 106, 116

pharmacist 116

Piazza San Marco 21, 82, 96

Pietà 35

places of worship 116

Po delta 70–1

Po valley 72–3

police 116–17

Ponte Coperto 66

Ponte dei Sospiri 27, 125

Ponte di Rialto 48

Possagno 66–7

post offices 116, 117

Procuratie Nuove 21

Procuratie Vecchie 21

promenades and squares 22–3

public holidays 114

Punte Alberte 72

radio and television 115

rail travel 105–6

Redentore 35–6, 102–3

restaurants 77–81

Rialto Bridge 48

Riva degli Schiavoni 22, 108

St Mark's Basilica 29–30

St Mark's Bell Tower 30–1

Salute 36, 114

San Cassiano 38

San Francesco del Deserto 62

San Francesco della Vigna 38

San Geremia 38

San Giacomo dell' Orio 38

San Giacomo di Rialto 38, 39

San Giobbe 38–9

San Giorgio dei Greci 39

San Giorgio Maggiore 39–40, 42

San Giovanni in Bragora 40–1

San Giovanni Crisostomo 41

San Giuliano 41

San Lazzaro degli Armeni 62

San Martino (Burano) 59

San Martino (Venice) 42–3

San Maurizio 43

San Michele 62

San Michele in Isola 62

San Moisè 43

San Nocolò dei Mendicoli 43

San Nicolò da Tolentini 43

San Pantalòn 43–4

San Pietro di Castello 44

San Polo 44

San Rocco 44

San Salvatore 44

San Sebastiano 44–5

San Stae 45

San Trovaso 45–6

San Zaccaria 45, 46

San Zanipolo (Santi Giovanni e Paolo) 9, 32–3

Sant' Alvise 36–7

Santa Maria Assunta 34

Santa Maria dell' Assunta 63

Santa Maria del Carmelo 33

Santa Maria dei Derelitti 35

Santa Maria della Fava 41

Santa Maria Formosa 42

Santa Maria del Giglio 35

Santa Maria Gloriosa dei Frari 33

Santa Maria dei Miracoli 35

Santa Maria di Nazareth 46

Santa Maria del Rosario 33

Santa Maria della Salute 36

Santi Apostoli 37

Santi Giovanni e Paolo 32

Santi Maria e Donato 62

Santo Stefano 45

Scalzi 46

Schiara Occid 75

Scuola di San Giorgio degli Schiavoni 50

Scuola di San Giovanni Evangelista 50

INDEX/ACKNOWLEDGEMENTS

Scuola di San Marco 50
Scuola Grande dei
 Carmini 49
Scuola Grande di San
 Rocco 49
scuole 49–50
sea, arriving by 106
senior citizens 117
shopping 83–8
 opening hours 116
sport and leisure
 activities 104
Squero di San Trovaso
 48
student and youth
 discounts 117–18

Tarvisio Forest 75

Teatro la Fenice 48–9,
 96
telephones 118–19
Tempio di Canova 67
tipping 119–20
toiletries 100
toilets 119–20
Torcello 62–3
Torre dell' Orologio
 20, 49
tourist offices 120
travel agencies 120
Treviso 65
Trieste 68

Val Tovanella 75
Valli di Comacchio 71
vaporetto 111–12

Venetian Lagoon
 14–15, 69
 map 58
Verona 65
Vicenza 65
voltage 110

walking in Venice
 112–13
water-taxis 105, 112
wildlife 69–76
Wildlife Oasis of Punte
 Alberte 72
words and phrases
 121–5

youth hostel 101

Acknowledgements

The Automobile Association would like to thank the following photographers and libraries for their assistance in the preparation of this book:

AA PHOTO LIBRARY Richard Newton took all the photographs, except for page 118/19 which was taken by Clive Sawyer.

GALLERIA DELL'ACCADEMIA 51 Arrival of English Ambassadors.

NATURE PHOTOGRAPHERS LTD 66 Corara Dolomites (N A Callow), 70 Black redstart (P R Sterry), 71 Grey heron (R Tidman), 72 Common tree frog (P R Sterry), 73 Little bittern (R Tidman), 74 Swallowtail larva (R Bush), 76 Birds-eye primrose (P R Sterry).

SPECTRUM COLOUR LIBRARY 10 Carnival, 29 Interior Basilica S. Marco, 52/3 Ca' d'Oro on Grand Canal, 60/1 Canal Murano, 63 Mosaic in Cathedral of Torcello, 64/5 Padua, 68 Roman Theatre Trieste, 104 Near Murano, 108/9 Riva degli Schiavoni, 117 Murano glass.

ZEFA PICTURE LIBRARY UK LTD Cover Grand Canal, 6/7 Restaurants along Grand Canal, 12/13 Doges' Palace, 20/1 Piazza San Marco clock tower, 26/7 Doges' Palace, 30/1 Piazza San Marco, 102/3 Regatta, 107 Isle S Giorgio, 125 Bridge of Sighs.

Author's Acknowledgements
Tom Pocock is grateful for help in Venice over a number of years to Dr Philip Rylands, the Director of the Peggy Guggenheim Collection, Mr Robert Morgan, Mr Jim Mathes and Signor Cesare Battisti of the Ente Provinciale per il Turismo.
During a final visit to check details before writing this book Tom Pocock was given generous hospitality by Magic of Italy Ltd at two hotels, the San Cassiano on the Grand Canal and the Quattro Fontane on the Lido.

> #### Country Distinguishing Signs
>
> On the maps, international signs have been used to indicate the countries round Venice.
>
> Ⓐ = Austria   ⒽⓇ = Croatia   ⓈⓁⓄ = Slovenia

For this revision: copy editor Jenny Fry; verifier Paul Murphy
Thanks also to Tom Pocock for his work on this revision